SECRETS

OF A

STEWARDESS

D1334866

SECRETS

OF A

STEWARDESS

FLYING

THE WORLD

IN THE 1980s

GRETCHEN RYAN

First published 2019

The History Press
The Mill, Brimscombe Port
Stroud, Gloucestershire, GL5 2QG
www.thehistorypress.co.uk

British Library Cataloguing in Publication Data.
A catalogue record for this book is available from the British Library.

ISBN 978 0 7509 8999 2

Typesetting and origination by The History Press
Printed and bound in Great Britain by TJ International Ltd.

MIX
Paper from
responsible sources
FSC® C013056

CONTENTS

Thank you, Mom, for teaching me to find humour in every situation, to value my friends and family and for instilling in me a positive attitude to life. You were the maestro!

This book is dedicated to everyone who perished in the Helderburg disaster. You have never been forgotten.

PREFACE

It was the 1980s, when all self-respecting women wore shoulder pads and legwarmers, possibly at the same time. Air hostesses, meanwhile, squeezed themselves into tight-fitting skirts and were weighed before every flight to make sure that, heaven forbid, they weren't too fat to fly. For the airline industry, it was a period of debauchery and there was a complete absence of political correctness. Amen to that!

Sexual harassment was not, as yet, a coined term. Discrimination was an undiscovered word. What a world it was! We had The Carpenters and Donny Osmond, Maggie Thatcher and feathered hair. Now that's what I call nostalgia.

Many readers will be horrified at what the rookie air hostess encountered at the hands of lascivious pilots. And please God, do not let any daughter of mine be subjected to those wandering hands. In today's world, a lot of the behaviour described would be liable to prosecution, but these anecdotes need to be seen in context. There will never be another time like that bygone era. And maybe that's not a bad thing! This was a time of excess, cleverly disguised as fun. Is it a sentimental yearning for the past, or is it simply the memory of youth, that makes the good old days seem so attractive?

Indeed, if you think the bankers or politicians were up to no good, you should've seen what was happening in airlines during that period. In fact, you'd be forgiven for thinking that some of the stories in this memoir were urban legends. But, believe you me, they happened! Just like when Jules, an obviously gay steward working in the business-class cabin, came swishing down the aisle, stopped beside a man and woman seated in his section and said, 'The captain has asked me to announce that he'll be landing this super colossal aeroplane shortly, my lovelies, so if you could just put up your tray tables, that would be abolsutely marvellous.'

On his trip back up the aisle, he noticed that the woman had ignored his request. 'Darling, maybe you didn't hear me over those naughty, noisy engines. I asked you to raise your trazy-poo. The main man is going to pop us onto the ground. in a seccie'

She turned to him and said, 'In my country I am called a Princess. I take orders from no-one.'

'Well, sweet cheeks, in my world I'm called a Queen, so I outrank you. Put up the tray, bitch!'

And just for the record … if anyone recognises themselves in this memoir, don't flatter yourself. It's not you. Even if you have the same name. It's probably just somebody who reminds me very much of you.

Also … if a few of the facts are wrong, well, that's just the way I remember it. After all, why let the truth stand in the way of a good story?

1

FASTEN YOUR
SEATBELTS

April 1983

It was essential to appear nonchalant about my new career. Soon I would be lunching on the Champs Élysées one day, whizzing down the slopes of St Moritz the next, before running with the bulls in Pamplona the following one. It was a well-known fact that an aircrew's idea of roughing it was anything less than a five-star hotel. I liked that philosophy.

My smoky-blue uniform hung from the cupboard door, covered in plastic. The wrapping was meant to deceive anyone who might enter my bedroom into thinking that I had not tried it on a 100 times already. It was the real McCoy. The white cotton shirt sat crisply against my skin. The skirt was snug. I buttoned up the waistcoat and only once I had slid my arms into the cool lining of the jacket did I look up. Nearly there. The silky orange, white and blue patterned scarf, loosely knotted, felt like soft ice cream around my neck. Dark stockings and navy blue high heels completed the look. The coup de grâce was when I pinned a shiny bronze wing to my lapel. A glamorous figure looked back at me from the full-length mirror with a mixture of pride and disbelief. Eat your heart out, Coco Chanel.

I had finally achieved my girlhood dream of becoming one of those most revered of all female species: an airline stewardess – the epitome of glamour and sophistication. Especially to one like me, who had grown up in a one-horse backwater farming community in a rural part of South Africa. Perhaps my view was skewed: I even thought the lady who collected our money at the local swimming pool was smart and sophisticated. Maybe it was the uniform.

My father clearly didn't share the same enthusiasm for my new career. He whinged about the fortune he had spent on my university education. 'You don't need a degree to become a "flying mattress",' he wailed, fuelling even more excitement in me. I had no idea when he had become an authority on the purported wanton behaviour associated with air hostesses. I had already disappointed him by not following the generations-old tradition of pursuing a profession in the law. That was what our family did. Just not me. I was about to spread my wings.

Four years at university had slowly integrated me into city life. I swapped my bare feet for sandals, traded frayed shorts for miniskirts and made new friends. However, despite this metamorphosis from country bumpkin to city girl, I was nowhere near as grown up as I was to become in the airline industry.

The day I plonked that mortarboard on my head and donned my black cape was the same day I was advised that my application for a role as cabin crew for South African Airways had been successful. As the chancellor of the university was about to tap me on the head, I said to him, 'I'm going to be an air hostess.' He looked horrified and brought the wand down with far more force than required. He would've been lethal with a samuraI sword. Just the thought of that made me rush my very unacademic legs right off that stage.

It was obvious that he shared the same attitude as my father. In their eyes, having a degree somehow put me in a superior bracket, not to be wasted on some frivolous occupation. Not to mention a job as immoral as the one I had chosen. I was far more excited about having made it into the airline than having a Bachelor of Arts degree bestowed upon me. It's not like I had a PhD in the mating habits of the Outer Mongolian muskrat. That was the advantage of doing such a general degree: I had no career path mapped out. And I had vaguely satisfied my parents.

Every time I saw a plane fly overhead, it gave me a much bigger thrill than walking into a lecture hall. That was enough to convince me that I was making the right choice. We all have to forge our own path through life. Sometimes, it takes a couple of attempts. I couldn't understand what the fuss was about getting a degree at all – anyone could do that. It was much tougher to join the airways. And it took almost as long.

The selection process was competitive and rigorous, though it certainly didn't entail anything even vaguely academic. That might have had something to do with the fact that the interview panel of three consisted of a retired pilot, a retired air hostess and a third person who very closely resembled a combine harvester. I don't think a single one of us was selected for our ability to speak foreign languages. We definitely weren't chosen for the capacity to regurgitate a mathematical equation of Einsteinian proportions. The main criteria was that we had to have the correct height to weight ratio. We also had to be fairly attractive

… and willing to plaster our faces with make-up. Our hair had to be tied into a bun so tight that it would have made the Botox brigade of today envious. They made us swear on the Bible never to be seen dead or alive with chipped nail varnish. Oh … and we had to show potential for being fun. I soon learnt to turn a blind eye to all forms of debauchery.

After four months of training, the day finally dawned for me to embark on my very first flight as a fully fledged crew member. I rose before the sun had even thought about it and got to work on my appearance. Cleaving a path through a steam-filled bathroom, I lined up the Dead Sea face mask and body scrub, triple-bladed razor, fluorescent-pink nail polish, facial-hair-removing strips robust enough to obliterate Saddam Hussein's moustache in one go, moisturiser, and enough war paint to frighten a Zulu warrior.

I was determined to allow myself enough time to get to the airport. The plan was to swan in gracefully on arrival for my first flight. I intended to look exactly like the elegant and beautifully groomed crew member who featured on the cover of that month's in-flight magazine, *The Flying Springbok*, with cheekbones to kill for, eyebrows arched to rival the Taj Mahal, and not a hair out of place. His name was Michael.

Now, I've done some stupid things in my life. Not stupid like Justin Bieber; everyone has the right to be stupid sometimes, but he just abuses it. This was more like clumsy – placing one high heel squarely in a mound of steaming dog turd on said morning. It took thirty minutes to retrieve my shoe. This was not part of the plan. As a result, I arrived with barely a minute to spare. Swear words rolled out of my mouth with more fluency than I had ever achieved in three years of French – that same French that had played no part in getting me into the airline.

I screamed into the parking lot at the Cabin Service building and scanned the sea of vehicles in search of a bay. All I saw were disabled parking spaces … another disabled slot … more disabled parking. Just how many quadriplegic air hostesses could there be? Believe me, I would have had more success trying to spot a unicorn. Finally, I found one – a parking bay, not a unicorn.

By now, my stream of invectives was like a river in flood. I threw the gear into 'park' and forced myself to have a quick look in the rear-view mirror. Thank God, the hair had survived the journey. I offered a silent prayer of gratitude to the god of hairspray. So far, so good. I lunged for my cabin bag on the back seat of the car, narrowly avoiding a potentially incapacitating incident, such as chipping or breaking a perfectly manicured nail. At the same time, I pulled the marginally lighter handbag over my shoulder. It was filled with enough cosmetics to open a small branch of Boots. With collarbones creaking under this heavy load, I waddled and wheezed my way into the building. Very attractive. I was ready to embark on my first flight.

As I entered, the room was abuzz with crew arriving from and going to various parts of the globe. Four chaps, blazers and ties cast aside, sat at a table playing poker, as they tried to while away a three-hour standby shift. They looked like they were having fun. I'd sooner chew my own hand off than shuffle a deck of cards.

Men and women minced around in spruce uniforms. High heels clicked on the tiled floors. Lipstick was applied. Hair re-plaited. Nails painted. The room abounded with activity, laughter and chatter.

I watched, fascinated, as bottles of strawberry champagne, apparently fresh off the supermarket shelves in Frankfurt, and Lindt chocolates from Zurich concealed in brown paper packets made their way discreetly through the sliding glass windows. A very receptive clerk grabbed them with the enthusiasm of a Jehovah's Witness inching a toe across the threshold. He was in charge of flight rosters. 'What's that all about?' I asked the crew member next to me, who was signing on for the same flight.

She positively oozed style – her make-up was immaculate, her hair was impeccable and her little body filled the uniform perfectly. Nobody could be that flawless and nice as well. I was right. She turned and looked at me as if I'd opened my lunchbox and let forth a foul smell of four-day-old egg. She took a step back. If looks could kill, she'd have been a weapon of mass destruction.

'You must be the new one on our flight,' she said, before striding off to check her locker. I'll bet that even Adolf Hitler got a warmer welcome at the Pearly Gates. Call me negative, but I didn't get the feeling that she was going to become my new best friend. In fact, I couldn't bear the thought of being on the same aeroplane as her. And I still couldn't figure out what I had done wrong in the first place.

A kindlier steward overheard this exchange and took pity on me. 'Ignore her, Doll. She's bloody Nora. I swear, if she had balls she'd have been the captain. We all do it. You've got to bribe these guys, if you want to get your flights. It doesn't always work, but it's worth a try.' He tossed a mane of thick, bleached hair, fluttered his hands, and whispered, emphasising every fourth or fifth word for effect: 'If you absolutely *have* to get somewhere, there's *one* way of guaranteeing it. Unfortunately, they're all straight – *fuck-all* chance for a queen like me to get a seventeen-day Perth!'

Once the entire crew had signed on, it was time for the next step … presenting myself in front of a 'check hostess'. We had to do this before every single flight. 'Standard procedure' they called it. God forbid your skirt stretched a little too tightly over a well-rounded tail, or a stray tendril found its way out of a chignon. Getting accepted into the airline was one thing; the hard part was to retain one's position. Not only did we have to appear glamorous at all times, but we had to maintain that height/weight ratio that got us into the airline, or else risk being shoved into the cargo hold of a jumbo jet and disgorged somewhere over an African desert in the dead of night. Comfort eating was definitely out of the question. It was easy to keep the height consistent, but losing weight after a weekend binge had its challenges. I scoured magazines for advice. 'Easy', they said, 'eat less, exercise more.' Yeah, right, and pay NASA to let you live in an anti-gravity chamber for the rest of your natural life.

There were a few psychotic individuals who actually volunteered for a career as this omnipotent being in the organisation. We lesser mortals only ever spoke the very words in a whisper, as if by saying 'check hostess' out loud you might be felled by a blow to the back of the head. In anticipation, I hauled a little stash of 'calmettes' out of my bag and headed for the drinking fountain. I was more petrified of this process than I would have been going to a gunfight armed with a plastic knife.

Stepping forward to show off my make-up, hair and nails, I knew I was starting to hyperventilate. It felt as though I'd swallowed a balloon. Ever a stickler for rules, I had substituted my au naturel look for heavy foundation and blue eye shadow, which left me closely resembling an exotic African lizard. I had tossed away my flesh-coloured lip gloss in favour of a bright red slash at the bottom of my face. The bun on top of my head was so tight that I found myself squinting through newly acquired almond-shaped eyes. My nails were pointy perfect. This was the easy part.

The other element of this checking process was worse. For anyone not hovering on the fringes of anorexia, it caused major angst. Fat arse never landed fair job. I sucked in my tummy and stepped onto the scales, suddenly feeling as heavy as if I'd eaten my twin sister. Nausea clutched at my stomach. I'd never been so apprehensive in my life. I kept repeating a mantra in my head, 'Please God, let me not be too fat to fly.' The well-groomed (whisper) 'check hostess' glanced at the scales before announcing, 'Hmmm … you're on the cusp. I'm not sure if I can allow you to fly.' Humiliation jockeyed for position with anger. Anger won; I pulled myself up to my full height, leaned over and, in one smooth action, plucked off her false eyelashes. I didn't really do that, but the feeling I got from just imagining it gave me an immense sense of satisfaction. Instead, I begged in a feeble voice, 'Please? It's my first flight.' She grinned, 'I was only joking. You're alright. Next!' It was pathetic to feel that elated at not being sent off to join the closest branch of Weight Watchers.

Next on the agenda was pre-flight briefing. The dimly lit, overcrowded little room had all the charm of a public urinal. Not that I noticed it. I was still on a high after being declared thin and gorgeous enough to fly. I practically skipped into the room. Richard introduced himself as our 'chief', the senior steward heading up the crew of four, with me as an extra. I was actually called a 'supernumerary', which sounded rather posh. I didn't have a clue what it meant, though.

'We've got a 118 pax,' he said, glancing at the sheet of paper in his hand. He had lovely, long, slim fingers, one of them adorned with a chunky, gold, signet ring.

'Packs of what?' I asked. I had visions of lugging 118 hindquarters of beef, wrapped in brown paper packages, up the aircraft steps.

'Pax. Passengers, Doll,' he answered. Patiently.

I saw madame of the earlier signing-on encounter roll her eyes and heard her mutter, 'Jesus.' Impatiently.

Richard continued, 'One UM.'

Didn't have the vaguest idea what a UM was but I would rather have taken my chances in a pool of piranhas than ask.

Next to me, Barry whispered, 'Unaccompanied Minor. Usually referred to as unaccompanied monster.' It all came back to me from my training. These were kids under 16, travelling on their own. You didn't want too many of these on a flight. I mean, I like children, I really do, but I couldn't eat a whole one.

Richard went on, 'One veg. No wheelchairs.'

Barry had become my new best friend, 'Vegetarian meal. No disabled passengers.' I squeezed his hand in gratitude.

'Anybody got any questions before we go?' Richard peered over his little round glasses. 'Righty-ho, then. We've got just under two hours to do a full breakfast service. Two tea and coffees, please.' He snapped his briefcase closed and we filed out of the door to the crew bus waiting outside the building.

It wasn't really a bus at all; it was a small white VW Kombi, which was already filled with another crew heading off on a different routing to ours. We squashed in. Everyone talked and laughed at the same time. I was thrilled to be part of this happy community. Despite the fact that I hadn't mastered the airline lingo well enough to even follow or contribute to the conversation, I still felt included.

'Three-two-five,' the driver announced, pulling up on the apron right beside a little Boeing 737. Affectionately called the 'Fluffy', an acronym for 'funny little ugly fellow', this plane was generally used for internal short-haul flights.

'That's us,' Richard said, and the five of us clambered over an assortment of legs and bags. 'Bye darlings,' he called over his shoulder as he exited. 'Knock yourselves out!'

In those days there was no passport control on local flights and crew weren't required to go through any security checks. We simply carried ID tags on us at all times, which we had to flash whenever asked to do so by an officious-looking security guard or immigration officer.

We lined up at the bottom of the steps that led up into the belly of the plane. An overweight, underpaid, disinterested security guard leaned against the railing, twirling what might have been a discarded plastic straw in his mouth, and said, 'Good morning. How are all of you today? Please would you be so kind as to allow me to inspect your identification cards.' Actually, he didn't say that at all. He just barked, 'ID.'

Richard flashed his card and sashayed up the stairs. Next was Madame whose blonde bob bounced closely behind him. As Kornelius, the other steward, climbed up after her, he snorted with laughter. I followed, and Barry picked up the rear. We all crowded into the small galley to find out what had tickled Kornelius. 'Look,' he said, holding out his ID card. There, instead of a photo of this handsome, blonde man with a bushy moustache there was a huge hairy baboon staring back at us. That's security for you.

Once we'd stopped laughing, we got to work 'prepping' everything for the service. This entailed removing metres of cling wrap off little containers of fruit, placing racks of hot breakfast meals in the ovens, tying together clusters of tea bags and emptying sachets of coffee into big, round pots. My father would have wept copious tears to see his daughter, with the university education, stringing together tea bags for a living.

Next on the agenda was for me to go and introduce myself to the captain. For the benefit of those lay people who have never been closely exposed to life in any airline, let me take this opportunity of explaining the hierarchy of deities inside an aircraft, in a bygone era. Before the emergence of low-cost airlines, when pilots became a dime a dozen, the minute the aeroplane doors closed God lost his rank. The captain immediately acquired the self-imposed status of the Father, the Son and the Holy Ghost, Allah, Jehovah, whoever. Now this is not to say that everybody viewed captains in this light. But they themselves certainly did. To be fair, they were a select group – highly qualified and mostly airforce trained. Each country boasted a national airline, and it was the highest privilege for a man with a full set of wings on his lapel to be able to represent the national carrier as a pilot. When this was combined with a full set of teeth, they were really appealing. But they were mainly attractive due to the status they held, power being the ultimate aphrodisiac and all that. Adding to their allure was the fact that, due to stringent six-monthly medical checks, they were in good shape physically. They relied on their youthful looks, combined with greying sideburns, as they strutted through airports around the world, a coat hanger shoved down the back of their necks to keep their broad shoulders pushed back, perceiving every glance in their direction as desire from the women and envy from the men.

I had been warned that some of these guys took themselves extremely seriously. Many of them were very easy on the eye, most of them were married and every one of them would try and get into your knickers.

More anxious than a ball boy at a John McEnroe tennis match, I stepped into the cockpit and said, 'Hello, I'm Gretchen.'

The co-pilot smiled and said, 'Johan.'

The captain, seated in the customary left-hand seat, turned to me and, in full hearing of his colleague responded, 'Gretchen, you are the first pregnant air hostess I've ever flown to Cape Town.'

'But Captain,' I spluttered, 'I'm not pregnant!'

He raised and dropped his eyebrows suggestively, gave me a lascivious grin and said, 'Ah, but we're not in Cape Town yet!'

I felt the flush spread up my neck and I knew my face was about to take on a very unattractive puce hue, despite the many layers of panstick. I fled out of that cockpit faster than it took a pilot to remove his wedding ring … but not quickly enough to miss the gruff laughter that followed. My confidence was shattered. It was round about the mark where you might expect to find a tapeworm doing the limbo. Low. Very low.

This was my initiation to the pranks played on new cabin crew on their maiden flight. I didn't know that I was being set up for a few more, which would make this first working flight of mine indelibly printed in my memory.

Once all the passengers had boarded, stowed their bags and fought over window seats, it was time to start the safety demonstrations. Because there were no individual in-flight monitors for each passenger, we had to do the full safety demo manually. So, I took up my position in front of the bulkhead, fully armed with a stock of seatbelts, oxygen masks and inflatable life jackets.

It seems like such a simple thing to do but, at the time, it left me with my heart pounding in my chest, as I stood at the front of the aeroplane with what felt like 45,000 eyes upon me. My arms were like lead, moving in staccato motions as I picked up the strip of seat belt. I smiled as graciously as I could and mastered a stare that did not make eye contact, but simply glided over the heads of passengers, while never letting that lipstick-painted smile fade. I felt like a fake, my outer confidence totally divorced from the inner turmoil.

I managed to get through the seat-belt demonstration without a hitch. 'Insert the flat metal tip into the buckle' – hard to mess up on this one. Mind you, it worked like every other seatbelt. If they didn't know how to fasten this themselves, they probably shouldn't have been out in public unsupervised. My confidence soared and I hoisted myself up a few inches.

'In the unlikely event of an explosive decompression, oxygen masks will be released automatically from the panel above your head. Pull the mask towards you and place it firmly over both nose and mouth, whilst breathing normally.' I yanked the yellow, plastic mask towards my mouth and demonstrated to all the bodies seated within my vision, exactly how it was to be used in an emergency. I wouldn't have shown up for this flight if I'd thought we were actually anticipating a decompression in the cabin pressure, but better to be safe than sorry.

Following the instructions over the PA, I then removed the mask from my face, placed it on the empty seat next to me in exchange for the life jacket, which was to be the last part of the safety exercise. 'If your life vest doesn't inflate, it is broken.

Oops. So sorry.' Like you're going to survive a ditching anyway. Of course the aircraft was equipped to land on water … but only once. When I turned to face my audience again, their laughter and clapping thundered through the cabin. Ah! They really liked me. Perhaps they knew it was my first fight. So, I grinned even harder, basking in this new-found affection and continued to exhibit the use of the life jacket in the event of a ditching.

The laughter continued. A little pig-tailed girl, a few rows in front of me, giggled as she cupped podgy hands over her mouth and stared straight at me. She needed a good telling-off. She was just plain rude. I tried to win her over by wrinkling my nose and winking at her in that embarrassing manner that one adopts with young children. This made her mother laugh, too. It was clear that neither of them was paying attention to the safety demonstration. Did they not understand that it was for their benefit? There might have been fifty ways to leave a lover, but there were only four ways off that aeroplane. And if they didn't sit up and take notice, I would not be showing them where those four emergency exits were.

Suddenly, I wasn't feeling so bold anymore. The smile felt like it was zig-zagging its way off my face. In my peripheral vision, I noticed a few crew members leaning out of the galley and looking up the aisle at me. I felt a warm glow at their support. It was good to be part of a team. I gave them a quick thumbs-up.

By now, my hands were shaking like a rattlesnake on a date. Despite the loss of fine motor control, somehow I pulled the bright yellow life jacket back over my head and replaced it in the little plastic pouch. I even managed to do this without dislodging the bun on top of my head. Granted, with all the hairspray and clips, it would have required earth-moving equipment to displace it.

After returning the demo equipment to the allocated stowage, I decided to take a quick breather in the loo, before joining the others in the galley. Once I had locked the door, I stared at my reflection, as involuntary tears of humiliation seeped from my eyes.

Around my nose and mouth – just where I had so conscientiously demonstrated the correct use of the oxygen mask – sat a bright red circle. Somebody had ringed the inner rim of my oxygen mask with lipstick.

Was there meant to be a funny side to this? I stormed into the galley and whipped the flimsy curtain closed behind me, to protect the passengers from my fury. I didn't care that I still had a red ring around my face – I would clean that up later. I was about to launch into my attack when Richard raised his perfectly plucked eyebrows at me and said, 'Jesus, Doll, you look like a thundercloud with a bone up its arse.'

I had to laugh. The image was so vivid.

'Sorry, Doll, it had to be done! Come on girls, let's get her cleaned up,' he said to the other two stewards. They grabbed my handbag and hauled me back to the loo, where they left me to repair the damage. Madame had disappeared back to her little sanctuary in business class. No help from her, then.

Fortunately, my sense of humour kicked in at this point, slightly warped as it may have been, thanks to growing up in a family where laughter and teasing had formed part of our upbringing. At least if you can laugh at yourself, you will always be amused.

With an additional layer of foundation and blusher, I returned to the galley to a conspiratorial hissing of sibilants as Kornelius said, 'You had a lucky escape, Babes. Yesterday, we put pepper into the new hostie's demo mask. She sneezed all the way to Durban. How was I supposed to know she was asthmatic?'

I loved the feeling of camaraderie amongst this crew and I knew that in a way they were testing me, not conspiring against me. The intention was not humiliation, just a good laugh for everyone. They had chosen their victim wisely. The thought did cross my mind that perhaps, on the return flight, we could repeat this little antic on the unsuspecting senior hostess up front who, so far, had not endeared herself to me and showed no potential for doing this for my entire airline career. Unfortunately, she was the untouchable one, who only read the announcements and would never deign to perform the actions. I got the very distinct impression that she was the kind of person who had no enemies, but was intensely disliked by her friends.

Finally, we were almost ready for take-off. The plane had been pushed back and the crew were running around latching stowages. Activity on a scale of one to ten was around fourteen. It was manic. My duty was to check that all the passengers in my section had paid attention to the announcements, followed the instructions and fastened their seatbelts. This required a confidence I did not yet possess. Cringing but conscientious, I walked down the aisle swinging my head from side to side, staring straight down into the crotch of every passenger, practically nose to groin. I could tell some of them thought I was a pervert. I was completely convinced of it by the way one man said, 'I think you're a pervert.'

Job done, I headed toward my jump-seat, finally ready to undertake my first official flight. Just before I could take up my position, however, Richard came to me and said, 'Doll, quickly go call Mr Mike Hunt in 13A. I'm going to upgrade him to business class. But hurry, we'll be taking off in a minute.'

I shot out of my seat – knowing that the plane was already being pushed back – and bolted down the aisle. Scanning the row numbers on the overhead stowages, with my head craned at an angle, I ran past Rows 10, 11 and 12. Then I got to Row 14. What had happened to Row 13, I wondered? The engines were powering up beneath my feet. I had to find this passenger quickly. I ran backwards and forwards in search of the missing row of seats. Eventually, as the engine noise grew louder and take-off was imminent, I hurled myself back into the galley, 'Richard, I can't find him. Where's Row 13?' I asked. The panic in my chest was exactly the same as I'd felt not long ago, whilst waiting to see if a second blue line would appear to mock me on the slim stick of the pregnancy-test kit. That kind of panic.

'There, on the right,' he indicated, waving in the general direction. 'Just call him; there's no time left. Move it, Doll!' I could just picture him placing those flawlessly manicured hands on his slim hips, in a gesture of total irritation, as I heard him add, 'Honestly, these new girls ...'

Barry nudged me, whispering, 'Go, Doll. Don't mess with an angry queen, ever.' So I put my dignity on hold and tore back down the aisle to where he had pointed. As instructed, I shouted out for the elusive passenger to identify himself.

I have never stopped reliving that moment of abject horror, which is as clear to me as if I was viewing it on a cinema screen. There I was, trying to look cool and sophisticated in front of a full load of passengers, eventually running around the cabin manically, shouting, 'Mike Hunt. Where's Mike Hunt?'

2

I'VE GOT ALTITUDE

With a couple more flights under my never-allowed-to-expand belt, my self-assurance was rocketing. There was no doubt that I had the appropriate disposition for the job. Oh yes, I could be counted on to participate in any crew-related activity that promised to be fun. And I did try to be nice to the passengers. As long as they weren't too demanding. If only they could've been a little more like the jet engines that ferried us through the skies, because at the end of a flight, at least the engines stopped whining.

As cabin crew, we were continually reminded that the passenger was always right and was to be treated accordingly. Easy for the head honchos to make that mission statement from the vantage point of a luxurious office block, with gold-plated urinals and satin-lined toilet paper, from whence they polished their anuses to a high gloss. Not so easy for those of us at the coalface, who knew better: not only is the customer wrong, he's likely to be ugly, rude, and have bad breath into the bargain.

The more flights I did, the more I learned. I soon became familiar with airline vernacular. In the days of exclusively male pilots, the flight deck was called the 'cockpit', sometimes, coarsely referred to as the 'snake pit'. Female cabin attendants were called 'air hostesses' which morphed into 'hosties'. Once you retired, you became a 'post toastie'. There were also labels according to the position we were allocated to work in, on any particular flight. If you were lucky enough to be the senior girl working exclusively in first class, you were known as the 'senior bag'. The most senior person in each section – first, business and economy class – was called the 'chief', be it man or woman. But the lowliest junior on a flight ended up at the blunt end of the aircraft, stuck in the galley, preparing endless pots of tea and coffee and running down each aisle replenishing items on the trolley. This person was appropriately known as the 'galley slave'. If you were the person saddled with pushing this fifty-kilogram wagon down the aisle and you ran out of coffee, you would signal this to the galley slave by forming a 'C' with a thumb and pointer finger. If you needed more tea, you would indicate this by making a 'T' sign, using both pointer fingers. And if it was milk you ran out of, you would simply cup both hands around your breasts.

There was another euphemism frequently used by cabin crew. 'Lunch box' was an indirect reference to the more offensive or blunt allusion to male genitalia comfortably ensconced behind the fly of a man's trousers. This term was favoured by both hostesses and gay stewards, as they prowled the cabin.

Petal was a senior steward, who had a penchant for expensive aftershave combined with a predilection for checking out lunch boxes. Petal was eccentric in his own right. Short, bow-legged and balding, with a ring of ginger hair around the perimeter of his head, a bulbous nose and a jovial attitude to life, he looked a lot like Tickey the Clown. Everybody who got to know him understood that the person allocated the position of galley slave on any flight on which he was the chief had to ensure that there would always be a pot of tea brewing. Where many crew snuck the odd alcoholic beverage, his main quirk was drinking endless cups of tea on board. His other quirk, however, was checking seatbelts. Normally, this task was allocated to the lesser-ranked members of the crew, but Petal insisted on doing this himself. 'I'll do the lunch box check, Doll – it's wasted on a hetero like you,' he told any straight steward. Sometimes, we followed him unobtrusively down the aisle, double-checking that our female passengers were strapped in, too, as he paid them scant regard, being sidetracked as he was by staring down into the forked part of the human body, between a pair of male legs. On many occasions he would race back into the galley, short legs pumping, and on the point of hyperventilating, say, 'Jesus, Jessie, check out the lunch box in 29A!'

On a Cape Town-bound flight, Petal was working on the one side of a trolley and I was on the other, as we handed out hot dinners – so hot that we had to use paper serviettes to manoeuvre them between the starter, dessert, bread roll and portion of cheese and biscuits on the blue, plastic trays. It was a tight fit and not always a perfect one. As I reached over, across the passenger seated in the aisle seat, C, to hand the handsome man sitting in the window seat, A, his meal, a traumatic incident occurred. The foil-covered pouch of roast beef in gravy slid off the tray and into his unsuspecting lap. The poor man screamed, as boiling liquid seeped like quicksand through his trousers and stained his crotch to a dark patch of molasses. His lunch box was scalded. I had obliterated his chances of ever reproducing;

I had deformed his sperm. They would no longer be healthy little tadpoles, but were now merely scorched seeds, drowned in Bisto.

I was mortified beyond the speaking of it. Petal's eyes sparkled. I mumbled an apology. Petal volunteered to clean him up. He raced back to the galley, grabbed a handful of blue and white absorbent paper towels. He was smiling at his good fortune – when last had he been able to legally place his hands on a passenger's scrotum, all in the name of service?

The man was magnanimous in accepting my apology. He was equally polite in declining Petal's kind attempt at rubbing him down and graciously accepted our offer of refunding his dry-cleaning costs. We all huddled in the galley afterwards as Petal explained to Viv, the galley slave who had missed the entire incident, and wanted to know what was going on. 'What can I say, Doll? His supper cooked his lunch.'

But Petal did not always exude the bonhomie of an antique's auctioneer about to close a deal with the bang of a hammer. He was notorious for throwing a hissy fit when exasperated by a full load of demanding passengers. Internal flights were filled mostly with white South Africans who, in those days, were accustomed to having servants fluttering around them. Some of them extended this attitude to airline crew, whom they similarly regarded as staff, purely there to react to their every whim. It was on such an occasion that Petal lost it. He stomped into the galley, his face flushed, the fringe around his otherwise bald head wafting like a haze of ginger candyfloss, and put out a hand. 'Silver salver,' he demanded. Somebody thrust the metal tray we used for carrying drinks to and from passengers into his stubby fingers. He promptly dropped the heavy platter to the galley floor, where it made a noise not dissimilar from a herd of buffaloes hitting a brick wall. Witnessing startled passengers involuntarily ejecting themselves from their seats was enough revenge for him. With his nose in the air he swished down the aisle, swatting aside groping hands as they clutched at the tails of his waistcoat to stop him and enquire about the explosion. 'What noise? Oh that? We just lost an engine. So–rree.'

The pranks on board continued at a rapid and steady rate, but so too did my learning curve. I was now complicit in immortalising these embarrassing capers. I developed a good eye for spotting anyone less experienced than me. Most probably out of a sense of nostalgia, my favourite was still the lipstick around the oxygen mask. It was such an easy one. I didn't make many friends, but I did laugh a lot. I even got bold enough to tease the cockpit … although I learnt that it was probably safer not to. They didn't like it much when the joke was on them. Maybe I just picked the wrong guys when I walked into the cockpit and confidently asked, 'What do you call a small pig?' 'A piglet,' one of them answered. 'And what do you call a small owl?' I continued. Both pilots looked at me as if I was dim. 'An owlet,' they both said. Neither of them could see where this was leading. 'And a small haemorrhoid?' Blank looks. 'A pilot!' I announced, laughing at my own joke. I think the reason they didn't find it funny was because the captain was only five foot two. And I suspect the co-pilot suffered from the pain associated with abnormally enlarged veins due to persistent increase in pressure inside the anal sphincter of his rectum.

We seldom got into trouble with the powers that be for straying from convention in airline procedures, as long as they didn't compromise safety. I can only assume that even they realised the boredom for passengers on a long flight. It gave me great delight to provide some light entertainment at the expense of a newer crew member than myself. I even got a few 'letters of compliment' from passengers who found fun in the shenanigans. Not once did I ever receive one for providing them with an outstanding service. I respected their attitude. It never crossed my mind that perhaps my level of service was not as high as my aptitude for mischief.

The opposite of a 'letter of compliment' was a 'please explain'. It was scary if you returned from a flight and found one of these little notes in your locker. It meant that somewhere along the line, you had done something to upset a passenger on a flight. This could vary, from refusing to serve them a second cup of coffee during severe turbulence for their own safety – they would not see it this way but, hopefully, the senior manager with whom you would have your conflab, would – to beating them over the head into a state of unconsciousness with that same coffee pot.

Sometimes, a logistical error could swoop in and you would find yourself accused of all sorts of heinous crimes, despite the fact that even when placed into a hypnotically induced state of altered consciousness, you bore no recollection of said crimes or passengers. This did not matter. 'Guilty until proven innocent' was the motto of the day. Remember, the passenger was always right. The only possible avenue of escape was if you could prove that you hadn't been on the flight, on which the incident occurred, at all. And even then you'd be met with a suspicious, glass-eyed stare. Which is exactly what happened to a colleague of mine, Steve. Despite providing proof that he had, in fact, been strapped into a jump seat in preparation for a landing in Durban at the time of the alleged incident on a Cape Town to Johannesburg routing, he nevertheless got the evil eye. Finally, still unwilling to concede from his position of authority, the Complaints Manager glared at him and said, 'OK. Just this time. But don't ever do it again.' Power corrupts; absolute power corrupts absolutely. Steve still ended up with a black mark against his name.

On the internal Boeing 737 pool, we flew in a 'block', which meant that we were on a monthly rotation with three other cabin crew members. This excluded new hosties or stewards on their first supernumerary flights, who were allocated flights randomly. On occasion, this rota would be thrown out if you were called out on standby, or needed to swap out a flight with somebody for whatever reason.

The gods must have smiled on me when I was allocated my first permanent crew. Mani da Souza was our chief. He was always referred to as Mani-da-Souza – never just Mani. Not that he would've been confused with anyone else called Mani, even if it was the most common name in the airline, which it definitely wasn't. *Everybody* knew Mani da Souza. A less-reverent man never walked this earth. Mani da Souza was small of stature and large of personality. He covered his bald head with a wig that resembled a coir doormat, and had a matching moustache. His pale green eyes betrayed his delightfully vulgar sense of humour. I loved him from the start.

I couldn't have been happier to see Barry's name as the second member on my crew sheet. I felt forever indebted to him for his kindness on my first supernumerary flight. As vile (and I mean this in the nicest possible way) as Mani da Souza was, so was Barry nice. He had a kind and gentle personality, and was always quick with a laugh and a helping hand. He had dimples so deep on either side of his face that you could bury a small baby in them. I'm sure you get the picture – Barry was happy. Always.

The other person on my first crew assignment would grow to become my best friend. Lizzy and I shared a love of adventure, a vague prowess at tennis and squash, and an affinity for pilots. The latter earned us the label of 'cockpit flies'. Justifiably so. You didn't have to be Nostradamus to predict that we were going to have our fair share of romance, disappointment and heartbreak, per kind favour of the boys in blue with their greying sideburns.

On our first flight together, Mani da Souza gave us a taste of what to expect under his rule. I was pushing the trolley down the aisle, eloquently calling out the familiar refrain to passengers on either side, 'Chiggenorbeef? Chiggenorbeef?' I wasn't really sure why we gave them a choice, as both tasted the same anyway. Clearly, we were in the airline business, not the food business.

A movement at the back of the plane caught my attention. When I looked up, Mani da Souza was flouncing down the aisle, from the opposite end, dressed in my full uniform, which I had hung up in the cupboard in exchange for the pinafore we wore on board. The only way I managed to complete the service with a straight face was by keeping my eyes on the foil containers of chicken and beef. The most annoying part about it was that he looked better in my own skirt than I did.

On a subsequent flight, however, he went a step further. He omitted my uniform and instead, appeared at the end of the aisle, hidden from the passengers' view, wearing only his shirt and waistcoat, shoes and socks. He had tucked his scrotum, as well as other stray bits between his legs, to reveal a neat triangle of pubic hair. Try and keep a poker face when your chief is prancing around the galley, pinching his butt cheeks together in order to keep his gonads to the back, insisting that, 'Really, I am a girl.'

Flying with Mani da Souza meant that every flight was a risk. Not in an aeroplane falling out of the sky kind of way, but in a fun situation turning into a disciplinary hearing kind of way. Something was likely to happen that might just possibly get somebody into trouble. But it was always worth the risk. He'd gotten away with it for twenty years.

He could be ruthless with passengers. During a bar service, a particularly annoying yuppie, with a superior attitude, asked which soft drinks we had on board. Mani da Souza rattled off, 'Coke, Sprite and Fanta.' 'Don't you have Appletiser?' the man asked. 'No,' Mani da Souza replied, 'Coke, Sprite and Fanta.' 'Grapetiser?' In a voice that could melt the solar ice caps, Mani da Souza said, 'Let me explain something, Sir, this is a 737, not a 7-11.' Yuppie settled for a coke.

We had great fun with the announcements. Most of the time, passengers didn't listen to them anyway. Even at the risk of being reprimanded, it was fun to test them. On another late-night flight heading back to Jo'burg, I was about to make the pre-take-off announcements when Mani da Souza said, 'Relax, I'll do them, Doll.' This gave me the opportunity of popping into the loo to adjust my make-up. As I applied my fourth layer of mascara, I hummed my way through the repetitive welcome speech crackling through the speakers. However, when it came to the standard, 'Please return your seat to the upright position' section, I almost poked the wand into my eye as he said, 'Please return the air hostess to the upright position.' As I stepped out of the cubicle, I was greeted with a round of applause from a few passengers who had, in fact, been paying attention.

His other favourite, instead of 'the smoking of cigarettes only is permitted', was 'the smoking of cannabis only is permitted'.

This one usually went undetected by passengers, but always gave the crew reason to giggle. After a particularly hard landing one day, he grabbed the PA from me and said, 'Sorry about that, Ladies and Gentlemen. I must point out that it was not the captain's fault. It was not the co-pilot's fault. It was the asphalt. And if we have any frequent flyers on board, you are entitled to claim extra miles for the three landings we just had.'

In contrast, an announcement that he was probably best remembered for was one he made after any particularly gentle landing. The cabin would always erupt in applause. They did that in those days – passengers clapped their hands, the decibel level a barometer of the rating of satisfaction. Or possibly relief. After one of these scenarios, Mani da Souza would always say, 'We appreciate your applause, but frankly, we prefer cash.' Not a single complaint in response. But not a single penny, either.

Mani da Souza always managed to get away with it – he had more chutzpah than Idi Amin. Either the passengers didn't notice it at all or, if they did, they laughed. The one and only time that she tried it, Lizzy wasn't so lucky … simply because we hadn't spotted the Head of Training board the flight. Introducing the male purser of our flight as 'Madame Lazonga' didn't appeal to his sense of humour. Ah well, you can't please everybody all the time.

It wasn't only cabin crew who suffered from lack of experience. Older air hostesses showed no mercy in their treatment of 'boy pilots'. These were the guys who had just achieved their lifelong dreams of becoming an airline pilot. They had to do a couple of supernumerary flights (just as we did) before they were allowed at the controls. Their position was in the right-hand seat of the cockpit. Praise the Lord, there was always an experienced commander in the left seat.

On a flight to Port Elizabeth (I'd been called out on standby, so I was not flying with my regular crew), I stood in the doorway of the cockpit, waiting for my turn to go and introduce myself. Jana, a hostess with many years of seniority, was in front of me. She had done the rounds. 'He's a hottie,' she whispered to me. 'Watch him blush.' Hitching her skirt up just slightly, she lounged against the doorframe. 'Jimmy,' she said, and the boy pilot looked around. She crooked her little finger and waved it back and forth gesturing him to follow her. He got out of his seat in the tight-fitting cockpit and crouching, his tall frame bent almost double, he stepped towards her. Then she said, 'If I can make you come with my little finger, just imagine what I could do with my whole body!' It's not attractive to see a grown man blush.

Jimmy was going to be flying this leg. This meant he would also be doing the landing. Fear seeped through me. If God had wanted us to fly, He would never have invented boy pilots. Jimmy's lack of experience could have had far more serious consequences than my lack of experience in serving tea and coffee. At least nobody got hurt if I screwed up. Just a few burns and a dry-cleaning bill, at worst. I knew that flying wasn't dangerous per se, but crashing certainly was.

I'm sure Jimmy tried his best but still, the runway came closer to us faster than it should have. He must have known, though, that the probability of survival was inversely proportional to the angle of arrival. Large angle of arrival, small probability of survival. We slammed into the tarmac. Every single oxygen mask dropped out of the panels above the passengers' heads. It looked like Christmas. The bright yellow plastic cups dangled from clear plastic cords. All that was missing was tinsel.

The announcement came over the PA, 'Ladies and gentlemen, we HAVE landed in Port Elizabeth.' A female voice yelled,

I'VE GOT ALTITUDE

'Jesus, I think I lost my coil!' That was me. I wasn't entirely sure if we'd landed, or been shot down. Whether it was out of relief or just a sense of humour, the cabin erupted in laughter.

Next, the captain's voice came over the PA. He sounded as if he had swallowed a frog. I'm sure all pilots must have had elocution lessons to perfect the seductive, gravelly voice. With a hint of laughter, he cushioned his co-pilot's mortification by announcing, 'Ladies and Gentlemen, any landing you can walk away from is a good landing.' Pearls of wisdom. Thank God, he didn't go on to say that a great landing was one after which they could use the plane again. Why should the unsuspecting passengers know that it was his co-pilot's first ever landing? None of their business really; they hadn't paid for inside info. And, to be fair, they hadn't even had to assume the brace position.

My stint on 737s literally flew by and soon the time came for me to convert to the Airbus A300. This was a bigger, squatter aircraft that carried more crew and thus, unfortunately for us, more passengers. New things to learn were mainly safety-related issues, such as where the different types of fire hydrants and spare oxygen canisters were located. There were also a lot more doors on this aircraft which – in an emergency – had to be opened manually, in a different way to those of the 'Fluffy'. The Airbus carried more cockpit crew, too. In addition to the two pilots, there was a flight engineer on board as well. This was a step up in my flying career.

Once a year, we got rostered for 'emergencies'. This meant that we did a refresher course relating to safety aspects of all the aircraft we were qualified to operate on as crew. Following this, was a rather taxing written exam consisting of … thirty multiple choice questions. Impossible to fail. It also entailed time in simulated emergency situations and ditching practice in the custom-made swimming pool. Exercises in the 'mock-up' were dramatic – you never knew just what phony predicament you were going to find yourself in. It always felt like a very real emergency situation, though, as flames literally leapt through the windows and blasts made your eardrums cave in, while smoke filled the cabin. I hated this – I had never been good at roleplay. Lizzy and I were always thrown in together as a team and, sadly, she was no better than me at it. As we went hunting for the 'sick, lame and lazy', neither of us could wipe the embarrassed grins from our faces as colleagues acted out insane scenes, ranging from hysteria to pretending to be engaged in joining the mile-high club at the time of the 'crash'. It was better under the disguise of a full-face smoke mask. Well, it hid my awkwardness, but caused acute claustrophobia, which led to me ripping off the mask and jumping down the escape slide without giving a continental about my 'passengers'. This did not stand me in good stead with the instructors and I was forced to repeat the exercise, or be grounded. Needless to say, in light of this threat, my acting skills at once improved to rival those of Charlie Chaplin. I started hurling 'passengers' down the chutes indiscriminately while, at the same time, yelling at them to remove all sharp objects from their person, lest they puncture the slide. I passed the refresher course, but never befriended the girl who broke her ankle at the bottom of the slide. I kept my job, she was grounded. No-one ever said life was fair.

Ditching practice during the summer months was fine, except for the fact that the lifejackets played havoc with our suntans. Ditching during the winter months made me understand why nobody survived a ditching in the ocean. If the impact didn't kill you, hypothermia certainly would.

Manny de Almeida was a good-looking chap, who joined the airline with me in 1983 as a steward and was part of my Ab Initio group during our training. Therefore, he was always rostered with us on these refresher courses, too. How could we have known then that many years later all his attempts at putting these emergency procedures to the test would prove fruitless, as he perished with the rest of the crew and passengers when one of our planes crashed just off the coast of Mauritius.

In the '80s, safety concerns revolved primarily around fires on board or electronic, mechanical and technical issues, rather than security. Our pilots were well-trained. Their main motto was, 'Stay out of the clouds. The silver lining everyone keeps talking about might be another airplane going in the opposite direction.'

The cockpit door was never locked and, on many occasions, passengers and crew had the good fortune of being invited in to experience the thrill of a take-off or a landing. The captain, in his customary seat on the left-hand side of the plane, always had a bird's eye view of passengers as they crossed the tarmac to the bottom of the rickety stairs, which led them up to the plane. This sneak preview gave him an ideal opportunity to scout the talent on board. So, when you, dear passenger, thought he was doing pre-flight checks, he was, but just of a different nature. Within seconds, the bell would chime in the galley and the purser would be called in, 'There's a young lady with a high, blonde ponytail and a (pretty much non-existent) red dress, who's just boarded. Ask her if she'd like to sit in the cockpit for take-off.' Purely for PR reasons, of course; anything to promote the airline. Funny how they never invited men or children into their domain off their own bat. The latter had to invite themselves. Although, it has to be said, they were magnanimous and never turned down a request. After all, the child may well have dragged a sexy mother along; pilots never missed an opportunity.

As it was my inaugural flight on this bigger and more exciting plane, our purser, Chaz, insisted on asking the captain if I could sit in on the take-off.

I was reluctant. 'You sure, Chazzy? This captain's not so friendly.' All I'd got out of all three of them when I went to introduce myself was a grunt from each.

'He's fine. He's just a bit shy because he stutters,' he said.

'Hmmm ... he seemed grumpy to me.'

'Go, Doll,' he said. 'Everything's done here. I'll man your jump seat for take-off.'

We both laughed. It was such an odd figure of speech for someone as delightfully camp as Chaz to use. He couldn't man anything.

I stepped into the cockpit and fastened myself into the spare seat next to the flight engineer. He gave me a wink and a smile, indicating that they were in the process of pre-flight checks. I was fascinated. This was nothing like our pre-flight checks. This was serious stuff. They touched, prodded and turned lights, flipped switches and fiddled with toggles. I had no idea how they knew the difference between any of them, but the three chaps remained silent as they completed their tasks. All we needed to know was the difference between a halon fire extinguisher and an oxygen canister. One was red, the other green. The colour coding helped to avoid unleashing a lethal dose of chemical foam into the mouth of a breathless passenger suffering from hypoxia. Or it was meant to.

After a short while, the captain turned to face the co-pilot and the engineer and this is how the safety checks proceeded that day:

Captain:	B..b..b..b..b..brakes?
First Officer:	Ch..ch..ch..ch..checked.
Engineer:	Ch..ch..ch..ch..checked.
Captain:	F..f..f..f..f..flaps?
First Officer:	Ch..ch..ch..ch..checked.
Engineer:	Ch..ch..ch..ch..checked.
Captain:	T..t..t..t..t..trim?
First Officer:	Ch..ch..ch..ch..checked.
Engineer:	Ch..ch..ch..ch..checked.
Captain (exasperated):	F..f..f..f..f..fuck the ch..ch..ch.. checklist. Let's g..g..g..go!!!

This must have been a one-off on any aircraft throughout the world. The captain, first officer and flight engineer all afflicted by the same speech impediment. They might not have been fluent conversationalists, but they certainly were skilled airmen. I got to know the flight engineer on subsequent fights. Not only did he have a debilitating stutter, but he had a self-deprecating sense of humour as well. He was quick to tell the story of how, before joining the airline, he had had aspirations of becoming a newsreader on TV. When, as expected, he was turned down for the job, he told everybody it was because he was too short!

3

LEG-OVER
OR LAYOVER

It was time for my first 'night-stop', also known as a layover. As always, despite my good intentions, I arrived on the wrong side of early for my flight. I hauled my Delsey out of the car boot and dragged it off to the elevators, like a reluctant cow on its way to the abattoirs, tugging from side to side. I entered Cabin Services, flustered and slightly dishevelled by airline standards, perfectly groomed by the normal barometer applied to land dwellers. Irrelevant. I would have to find the time – of which I had none – to dart into the loo to make a few adjustments, before venturing within a 100 metres of a (whisper) check hostess. But, first, I needed to sign on for my flight. This is where the trouble began; a stand-by had already been called out in my place. She was definitely not elated. I could tell by the way she kept calling me 'Bitch'.

Being late or booking off sick – even if it was to have an arm amputated – was never a good move. It was right up there with eating meat on a Friday in my Catholic youth, tantamount to committing a mortal sin. The stand-by hostie continued to glare at me with such hostility that, given the choice, I would rather have stood in front of the above check hostess with no make-up on. She made me feel that I had been put on this earth to suffer and that this situation had been sent to me as some kind of penance. A real old sourpuss, she'd definitely missed her vocation in life. She'd have been better suited to a job as a mortician than an air hostess. Perhaps she realised this herself and so began flying with the intention of balancing her innate morbid nature with an intention to have fun, travel and make friends. I had a definite feeling the fun and friends were just never going to work out for her.

'Sort it out,' she said, 'because I'm not going.' She put her hands on her hips and thrust her chest forward. Her breasts strained against the uniform shirt like party balloons. My size 34As retreated into my bra, like nervous dwarfs peeking above the rim of a teacup.

There was nothing for it but to fix the situation. No way was I going to miss out on my first night-stop. I'd heard all about the glitzy, four-star Malibu hotel on the Durban beachfront. But, more importantly, it was up to me to resolve it – or risk a slow death at the hands of a disgruntled mortician–cum–air hostess, I feared.

Together, we marched off to the roster clerk. The process was reversed. Without so much as a 'Thank you', I'll have you know, she stomped back to her card game. I could swear I saw her replace a machete in her handbag. Clearly, she had better things to do than spend the night in Durban. I couldn't help feeling sorry for the poor sod with whom she was going to be doing those better things. Well, I can't take responsibility for the world's problems, can I?

I made a detour to the ladies'. Damage control required more time than I had available. Hairspray and lipstick would have to do. With an air of defiance, I strode towards the check hostess. I didn't recognise her, but she looked as if she ranked higher on the wickedness scale than Omaima Nelson, who cooked her husband and ate his ribs with BBQ sauce. To her credit, all she said was, 'Your hair's a mess. Promise me you'll redo your bun.' I agreed in much the same way I imagine Robert Mugabe promised a free and fair election.

After that little unexpected reprieve, I had to get my skates on to catch up with the rest of the crew. By now, though, my hair was practically flopping around my face like a kitchen mop on an aircraft carrier. When I finally hooked up with them, I was flustered, but delighted to find that Kathy was the senior bag on this flight. She was very easy to talk to and never discriminated against the younger and more inexperienced girls, like me. Everybody liked her. I'd done a few flights with her before and discovered that she was a keen runner. I didn't know then that we would become very close friends and spend many hours pounding the pavements of Johannesburg, London, New York and various other cities and islands together over the next twenty years.

We went through the routine checks and pre-flight briefing before boarding the plane for the hour-long flight. I went to introduce myself to the cockpit crew as usual. Hmmm … attractive. And young enough to possibly be unmarried. I envied the girls who were involved with pilots – all the romance at exotic locations around the world. I could picture myself linking arms with one of these gorgeous creatures with the silver sideburns, as we ambled along 5th Avenue in New York, or Hong Kong harbour. Perhaps even the Durban esplanade this very night.

They had already completed their pre-flight checks and were relaxed, wanting a cup of tea. Did I imagine it, or was that a wink from the main man on the left? My heart rate increased slightly as I stared back at the sunburnt laughter lines, which crinkled slightly around the most outstanding steel-grey eyes. My smile was as weak as my knees. Was I on the verge of having my first date with an airman? Confession: as I was single anyway, I did ask in my prayers every night for the powers above to send a man into my life and, if at all possible, I mean if it really, really didn't matter to Him, please could that man be a pilot. So, thank you, Lord, for your kind attention to this matter.

I returned with the tea. I had no problem handing the first officer and engineer theirs, but on addressing the captain, the cup rattled in the saucer as nerves and excitement got the better of me. He must have noticed this and, realising that I was still pretty new to this game of flying, said conversationally, 'Gretchen, I bet you a 100 rand that I can touch your boobs without you feeling it.' Ah, I was right. He WAS flirting with me, even if he was being a bit forward in front of his colleagues.

I laughed, pretending not to be flattered by the attention. 'I'm not as new as you think I am, Captain. I'm wise to all your tricks.' It felt odd calling him 'Captain' then when, later that evening, I would more than likely be calling him all sorts of pet names. 'Okay, then,' he replied, 'close your eyes.' With my new-found confidence, I complied. I'd been in the airline long enough now to foil another antic reserved for a newbie. However, before I knew it, he was vigorously fondling my breasts.

'Hey, I felt that!' I screeched, pulling backwards and almost flinging myself right through the cockpit door.

'Okay, you win. Here's your 100 rand,' he said, pretending to reach for his wallet. Bastard! And I thought he'd been flirting with me! If that had happened to me today, I would have ripped his voice box out with my bare teeth. But back then, all I did was giggle embarrassedly and disappear into the loo, until my cheeks stopped burning with humiliation. I did ponder whether to kill myself then, or wait until after the flight. And I refused to enter the cockpit for the rest of the trip. They could all die of thirst as far as I was concerned. So much for my first romantic encounter with an ace. Fucking arsehole. I didn't usually use that language, but for him I'd make an exception.

This was my lucky day. Not. We were in for a delay. Yippee – more time for me to be exposed to Pontius the Pilot. He'd already nailed my heart to the cross. What next?

Johannesburg is situated almost 1,700m above sea level. Being 'high' and 'hot' makes this one of the most challenging airports in the world. Now, in layman's terms, this means that the aircraft usually needs more distance to take to the skies due to the thin air. If you have ever wondered about the length of the runways at what was then known as Jan Smuts Airport, the thinner air was the reason for this. Now, while I might have forged some very close relationships with a number of pilots during my airline career, they didn't generally educate me on the technicalities of flying. But even I understood that there was some sort of correlation between the weight of an aircraft and the temperature on the ground. Something about lift, getting beyond the point of no return and aborting. Believe it or not, I'm still talking about aeroplanes here. Perhaps all this sexual innuendo had an influence on their choice of career. Many pilots seemed to think they could treat hosties in the same way they treated an aeroplane.

Anyway, on this particular day, just when I thought we were ready to close the doors and prepare for take-off, the loadmaster stepped on board with a sheet of paper covered in graphs and perplexing curved lines. He told the skipper that we would need to wait for the temperature to drop by at least two degrees, before we could take off. It seemed we had two choices: either we could hang around for an hour, or we could ask ten passengers to voluntarily offload themselves and their luggage and take a later flight out of Johannesburg. No one volunteered. Funny that. Well, he could have made everyone sweat it out on the plane but, instead, he suggested that the passengers disembark and rather wait in the air-conditioned lounge. They would be called to board once it was deemed cool enough to take off.

Most of the passengers climbed down the steps and walked across the tarmac to the terminal building. The crew stayed on board. So did about five passengers, whom I failed to spot at the time. As I was walking down the aisle from the back galley, I noticed the on-board music had been turned up loud enough to blast a bat right out of hell. I recognised the Afrikaans song, which was a big hit, by a famous South African crooner. He was known in the tabloids not only for his voice, but also for his superior attitude and lust for young, beautiful women. I definitely was not a fan. The voice bellowing through the speakers reminded me of a movie I'd seen where an innocent man was being burned with a blow torch. As I was about halfway down the plane, just near the emergency exits with the lovely seats that everyone requested due to the extra legroom, I bellowed out, 'Ah, my ears! Switch off that crap!' I noticed a movement on my left, turned and looked straight into the eyes of the acclaimed chanteuse, whom I had not even noticed boarding the plane in the first instance. Clearly our chief had and was attempting to flatter him by broadcasting his voice through the entire cabin. Talk about putting my foot into my mouth! I wondered briefly whether, if I ate myself, I would disappear altogether. But maybe I would become twice as big! I was saved from trying to extricate myself from further embarrassing apologies by an announcement that the passengers were boarding. I did actually wonder afterwards if the insult hadn't been lost in translation, as this Lothario of the music world didn't seem to be in the least offended. In fact, he was charming.

Kathy decided that, as it was my first night-stop, we had to do something memorable instead of just going to a restaurant in town. Thank God for Kathy. And she didn't even know that my hopes of romancing an aviator that evening had been dashed before we'd even gotten off the ground. We were going to have a beach barbeque. But this was going to be a beach barbeque in style. No paper plates or plastic cups for us. Remember what I said about air crew roughing it?

She managed to convince her fellow first-class crew that it was a rare treat, not to be missed out on. It didn't take much coercion. The purser, Hector, even suggested she make a list of what we'd need.

Digby faffed about selecting a couple of blankets from empty seats – unused and still sealed in plastic. We gathered together porcelain plates, stainless steel cutlery, glass rummers and wine glasses, porcelain salt-and-pepper cellars, linen serviettes and finally, as many miniatures, mixers and the odd bottle of wine as we reckoned we could fit into our respective cabin bags. Now, I know this might sound a lot like pilfering (I feel my conscience nodding vigorously) but, for some reason, back then, the attitude was that all those stocks had been written off already. Passengers were at liberty to take any of those items off the plane with them – the whole enchilada. Everything had already been accounted for and every single item that wasn't used, was discarded on return to base. Each flight departed with a new set of absolutely everything. The waste was horrific. Crew frequently threw away items in a bin, rather than go to the effort of unlatching stowages and returning the stuff. We convinced ourselves that we were actually doing them a favour by lowering the workload of the ground and cleaning staff (conscience nods furiously).

At the end of the flight, we disembarked all the passengers. Crippled under the weight of our 'in-flight shopping', we boarded the bus which ferried us to our hotel in the city.

So much for me luxuriating in the lovely hotel, with sea views to die for, failing the date with a pilot. Oh well, I told myself, there'd be lots more opportunities in the future. 'Carpe diem', as Robin Williams said in *Dead Poets Society* – that was my motto. We wasted no time checking into our rooms, just disappeared for a quick change of clothes and met up in the foyer a short while later.

'We need to get a car,' Hector said. He was right. But even if he wasn't, nobody was going to argue with Hector. Well, perhaps someone like Mike Tyson wouldn't fear 150kg of muscle that made up this short, stocky man, with the smiling round face. He looked a bit like Buddha. I have to confess, I did wonder – albeit briefly – in the event of things taking a turn for the worse, would he be able to go skinny-dipping? I mean, honestly, can a fat person skinny-dip? It just didn't sound right.

There was no choice other than to hire a car for the short journey. Public transport was not an option – mainly because it didn't exist – and taxis would swallow up twice our annual salaries.

Thank goodness for the Avis office in the hotel foyer. Armed with keys, maps and all our booty, we squashed ourselves into the little Fiat, like melting marshmallows. Hector had chosen the smallest vehicle known to mankind. He occupied most of the right-hand side of the car, while Digby was in the left front seat and Kathy and I were compressed into half of the back row behind him. For some reason, this intense discomfort made us laugh all the more. It had all the makings of an adventure. I've never been able to put my finger on exactly what it is that makes air crew such an upbeat bunch of people. Perhaps it's the idea of being paid to have picnics on beaches, instead of slogging away in an un-air-conditioned office putting your actuarial science degree to the test working out loss adjustments, premiums and ratios. But let's be fair here, that is probably what puts a smile on some people's faces. Just not mine. Don't let me ever be accused of professional envy.

'Where to?' asked Digby, who had assumed the role of navigator from the comfort of his single seat, as the car scraped over a speed bump.

'Thompson's Bay is stunning,' Kathy said, 'near Ballito. There's a tidal pool.'

'I remember going to Sheffield Beach as a child,' I said. 'There are loads of rock pools and caves.'

'Ah, a cave is what we need,' Hector piped up. 'In case it rains.'

Along the way we stopped to buy some foodstuffs, a grid for the meat, a pot in which to boil potatoes, kindling, candles and matches. Providing much amusement to the local kids, we poured ourselves back into our little matchbox car and set off for the final leg of the forty-five-minute journey.

The closer we got to our destination, the more threatening the weather became. But we were not going to let this affect our plans for the evening. The sun, fighting for position amongst the clouds, was just setting as we arrived at Sheffield Beach. The sea had a pinkish hue and the water that lapped the beach and trailed over sand, before it was pulled back into the ocean, shimmered gold and orange. There were rock pools and secluded coves, as well as big rocky outcrops with hidden caves. One got the sense of it being a bit wilder than other areas might have been. A few seagulls argued over a long-dead fish skeleton, their raucous cries cutting through the atmosphere. There was not a person in sight. Possibly this had something to do with the large black cumulus clouds on the horizon.

We carted all our goods from the car to the beach and set about preparing for our picnic. We laid out blankets, put out plates, filled our glasses and lit our candles. The salt spray from the sea clung to my hair. The air was filled with the pungent smell of seaweed. I lay back on the blanket with my feet in the soft sand and watched the last bit of colour retreat from the sky. A well-deserved rest after an entire hour of work on the plane journey from Johannesburg to Durban.

When the first few drops of light rain fell, we were not deterred; we simply decamped to one of the caves in the rocks, where we built our fire, huddled close together and marvelled at the smell of the meat as it slowly sizzled on the flames. But this halcyon ambience was to be short-lived, as a gentle breeze forced the smoke to keep changing direction. The wind got stronger and the smoke got thicker.

The rain started falling fast and hard. The fire went out. The blankets got wet. Digby tossed the potatoes out of the pot and used it as a pith helmet instead, to protect his bald pate from the deluge. Thunder roared. Lightning struck. It was time to go.

We moved like poo through a goose – hurried, but calm. By the cursory light of a couple of matches lit in rapid succession behind cupped hands, we managed to gather together every last porcelain plate, salt-and-pepper cellar, glass, piece of cutlery, bottle, serviette and food. We put it all in the blankets, which the two men hauled over their shoulders á la Santa Claus, and headed down the beach to the carpark. Water gushed off our heads and ran in rivers down our backs. South Africa is not known for light drizzle.

'It's going to be a schlepp sorting out all this stuff when we get back to the hotel, isn't it?' I said, flinching at the idea of unpacking sandy blankets, dirty glasses, wet linen napkins, crockery and cutlery. It was intended to be a rhetorical question.

'What stuff?' the other three asked in unison, as they tossed the blankets, with all their bounty, into the giant bins at the edge of the carpark. They raised empty hands to the sky, nudged each other in the ribs with their elbows, grinned and asked with innocently furrowed brows in mock confusion, 'What on earth are you talking about?'

I was astonished, shocked, horrified, both by their actions, as well as the fact that I was in total agreement. What was happening to me? How could I be in awe of their aplomb and admire the air of entitlement they exuded? What about my wholesome upbringing? The speedbumps on the journey home were a lot less noticeable, as we returned substantially lighter that we had arrived.

Not long after the Durban beach barbeque episode, Lizzy and I found ourselves on a layover in Cape Town. For those who have not visited this oldest and arguably most beautiful city in South Africa, put it on your bucket list. With Table Mountain at its heart and two magnificent oceans at its feet,

Cape Town is breathtaking. Majestic rocks and mountains hover over turquoise seas. Roads wind around hilltops, high above white beaches and vibrant harbours. Slowly rotating cable cars climb to the apex of the mountain, offering sweeping views of this cosmopolitan and eclectic city. Boats ferry people to Robben Island, the notorious prison that once held Nelson Mandela.

The people are colourful, their ancestry dating back to the arrival of Jan van Riebeeck in 1652 and the import of slaves from Indonesia and Madagascar. Along with these Dutch settlers, a range of useful plants were introduced to the Cape, including grapes, cereals, apples and citrus, which had an important and lasting influence on the societies and economies of the region. The area is well known for its vineyards that continuously produce award-winning wines.

The Cape hovered between Dutch and British rule, until Cape Town was finally ceded to Britain in the Anglo Dutch Treaty of 1814. But it was only in 1961 that South Africa gained total independence, severing all formal ties with Great Britain.

We stayed in The Heerengracht, a posh hotel in town. Despite its five-star status and luxury interior, the bedroom walls were thinner than a chameleon's eyelids. Acoustics in Pollsmoor prison had to have been better. There seemed to be more crew than paying guests in the hotel. I can only assume the sound quality had something to do with it.

That evening, a group of us met up in the foyer. Lizzy, another hostie called Karen, and I chatted as we waited for the cockpit crew to join us. To my abject horror, the first person to stroll towards us was Peter Shepperton, the very same arsehole (exception granted for foul language, as per the previous occasion) from my first Durban night-stop flight –

the one who had fondled my boobs shamelessly and now did not even recognise me. Dear God, where was a raptor when you needed one, or even a magpie, to peck out those steel grey eyes? As he put out his hand by means of introduction, he did not even make eye contact with Lizzy or me. Wanker. But, he positively salivated as he asked Karen her name and told her his. He was riveted by her bee-stung lips, blonde hair and double Ds. Before I could warn her about him, I could tell she had already succumbed to his charms. It had absolutely nothing to do with rejection, let me be totally clear on that. I was a young woman of substance who did not need this ... this ... MAN ... to make me feel complete. It's not as though I was still smarting from his rebuff; I was simply concerned about the emotional scars she might suffer on finding herself in bed giggling and having sex with this duplicitous character later in the evening, only to be forgotten before dawn. They're still married to this day.

The two pilots from our flight, Dave Appleton and Charlie Hendricks, joined us shortly afterwards. Fortunately. Otherwise Lizzy and I would have had to spend the entire evening watching the new lovers – like two turtle doves doing a display on a window ledge, cooing and bowing and (almost) jumping on top of each other, one's beak firmly attached to the other's neck. She was acting all coy, simpering like a little bird with a broken wing that couldn't fly, or couldn't sing. Made me feel like killing the effing thing.

The chaps had already discussed the plans for the evening. They couldn't have chosen a better venue. We took the scenic coastal train ride out to The Brass Bell – a little restaurant right on the sea in a tiny harbour village called Kalk Bay. Kalk Bay has a fascinating history that dates back to 1742, when the Dutch East India Company used it as a mini port. Later on, it became popular for its fishing that attracted families from diverse places such as the Philippines, Malaysia, Java and Batavia, many of whose descendants still live there today. As the population grew in this little fishing village, a railway line was introduced and the town rapidly expanded, which eventually led to the construction of the Kalk Bay tidal pools. A concrete structure was built for women to use as a changing room. It included a tea room which, in time, became the now well-known Brass Bell.

Situated on the side of the railway track, we literally stepped off the train and into the restaurant. Surrounded by rolling waves splashing against the plastic-sheeted windows, this little nugget nestled into the walls of the tidal pool. Every so often, I felt a bit of salty water land on some part of my body, while the smell of the sea zoomed up my nostrils. It was unique; I absolutely adored it and would come to frequent it many more times on subsequent visits to Cape Town.

We returned to the hotel quite late, but that didn't deter us from having a nightcap from the mini-bar in Charlie's room. By now, we had lost Romeo and Juliet. Our tongues were loose and our voices loud, but not loud enough to drown out the noise coming from the room next door … as if we hadn't had enough lust and pheromones bombarding us all evening. The four of us tried to guess whose it was. We soon found out. A bed frame banged against the wall. At frequent intervals, a woman's husky voice roared, 'Oh, John! Oh, John!'

The following morning, we all met up for breakfast in the hotel's dining-room. When the pilot in question – who had been the subject of the amorous activity the night before – entered the breakfast room on his own, everyone bellowed out,

'Oh, John! Oh John!' Totally oblivious to our derisive tone, he simply responded with a nonchalant wave of his hand and said, 'Hi guys,' then promptly sat down and ordered breakfast.

4

HAPPY LANDINGS

The time finally came for me to move on to the international routes. I'd served my term on the internal and regional pools. No pun intended. Don't get me wrong, I'd had more than my share of fun during my first five months of flying, but this, after all, was the reason we all joined the airline – to travel. Not, as I had predictably answered in my initial interview, 'Because I like working with people.' Bollocks! Nobody in their right mind would ever choose to deal with the public, especially when confined to a tin can at 35,000 ft with no eject button.

Being let loose on these much bigger planes entailed a more comprehensive conversion course than I had previously undertaken. It almost threatened to shock my grey matter into action, after having been dormant for about six months. The international fleet was varied: there were Boeing 747s, known as Jumbo Jets, Boeing 747 SPs (special performance), the 747 Combi that was used for a combination of passengers and freight, and then there was the 747-300 SUD (stretched upper deck). Each of these planes had its own unique set of emergency procedures, which you had to be able to recount without as much as a nanosecond of hesitation if woken at the stroke of midnight, or any other ungodly hour. My father would have been delighted to think that finally he was getting some value out of the money he had paid for my education.

These aeroplanes required a far bigger contingent of crew, varying between eleven and thirteen cabin crew and a minimum of five cockpit crew. Lizzy and I were delighted at the prospect of a greater selection of pilots on each flight. She and I soon discovered that in the airline, there were two opposing camps. We had to decide which group we wanted to ally ourselves with on the layovers. On the one wing, were the good-looking, testosterone-fuelled, gravelly-voiced pilots and, on the other, a collection of camp air stewards with the most wicked sense of humour. Both offered the opportunity of fun. The downside was that the pilots were married and the stewards were gay.

There wasn't much love lost between these two groups. When provoked, the latter had the ability to retaliate with a tongue so sharp you could cut open a cadaver with it. 'Bitch,' they would hiss if in any way offended by a butch male – be it a pilot or a passenger. But the boys in blue – up front in the sharp end of the plane – weren't stupid. They soon learnt that you never annoyed the person who served you your meal. Eye drops were the favoured weapons of reprisal. Word spread quickly amongst the cockpit crew. A couple of drops of Spersallerg inadvertently ingested resulted in frequent, violent and most definitely non-solid bowel movements.

On board, however, there was an enforced level of respect. No one would contemplate addressing the commander – to his face, anyway – as anything other than 'Captain' or 'Skipper', irrespective of your relationship with him. Some of these guys could be real arrogant jerks, with egos the size of a 737, who basked in their imposed status. They probably wouldn't have minded as long as the affronted steward had said, 'Here's your tea with eye drops and two sugars, Oh Captain, my Captain.' It was common knowledge that the only difference between the Pope and a pilot was that the Pope only expected you to kiss his ring.

Behind their backs, we sometimes referred to them as 'Beulah Bangles' due to the conspicuous gold rings around the cuffs of their uniform blazers. Captains were graced with four of these golden hoops around their sleeves. Co-pilots, who only sported three, were labelled 'Hetty Help-me' and the less glamorous flight engineers, with purple stripes in between the two gold rings, earned the name 'Sally Switchboard'.

As opposed to the short one-night layovers on the internal flights, international slippings (days away from base), could be as long as seventeen days. Whether one night, five, seven, ten or seventeen, this always presented an opportunity for a good old shindig and a few romantic dalliances. It was a common perception that the airline flew crew from one festivity to the next. Based on first-hand experience, this perception was probably not unjustified. After all, nobody travels all the way to Europe, America or the Far East for an early night and a cup of cocoa.

My first international flight was to London. Johannesburg/London was one of the airline's most lucrative routes, resulting in two flights a day, which meant your chances of being scheduled to fly to the UK reasonably often were good.

The Jumbo Jet seemed enormous in comparison to the little Fluffies and Airbuses. So many crew! And so many passengers! I was already tired and all we had done was board the passengers, directed them to their seats and assisted with stowing their oversized hand luggage. I stood by silently and watched as a large man, with even larger sideburns, tried to stuff an enormous bag into an overhead stowage. Even blind Freddy could've seen that it was never going to fit. I approached him and told him I'd need to take it off him and hand it over to the ground staff to check in. He was furious, 'When I fly on other airlines, I never have this problem.' I smiled sweetly at him and replied, 'Sir, when you fly on other airlines, I don't have this problem either.' Now hand over the bag, Prick. But I had made up my mind that I was not going to allow anything to get to me in return for the privilege of flying to London – I would be patient, courteous and understanding. I couldn't promise that my renewed attitude would last for the duration of the entire flight, though. But it was a good start.

Gazing down the full length of economy class was like looking at a sea of turtles, heads bobbing up and down. There was a set routine to the service procedures, which started with handing out menus and hot towels. On a full plane, this took an eternity. People weren't always sure what the purpose of the little scented cloth was. It didn't take much to confuse passengers. Sometimes I was convinced that half of them were illiterate and the other half couldn't even do long division. A woman, with pendulous boobs and a tiny brain, took one gingerly in her fingers, while all the time looking at me as if I was a bit slow. 'What's this for?' she asked. I couldn't tell if she was always that stupid, or if she was making a special effort on that particular day, but I was tempted to tell her that if she rubbed it across her forehead a couple of times, she might increase her IQ to that of a halfwit. No sooner had we handed them all out, than we had to start the procedure of collecting all these soiled bits of rags which, by the looks of them, some people had washed themselves with, cleaned their shoes with and finally given a good, old nose blow into. You couldn't beat the glamour of the job.

The next part of the service consisted of pushing a trolley, filled with cheap, little, plastic-string headsets, down each aisle and try to convince passengers to buy these objects of torture. They had to squash the huge, rubbery earpieces into their ears. Nothing like the foam-padded, Walkman-style earphones of today. Not one of us mentioned the resulting earache, or the fact that they wouldn't be able to hear a thing through these anyway. I pushed sales hard. I was on commission, after all. One passenger had clearly tried these earphones before, as he responded, 'No thanks, I don't think I'll need any of those this evening.' What he meant to say was, 'Fuck off with your cheap crap!'

There was a downside to these headsets from a crew perspective, too – it wasn't only passengers who suffered the irritating consequences. In order for it not to keep popping out, the earpiece had to be shoved deep into the middle ear, almost to the point where you would perforate the eardrum and allow the cable to start travelling down the Eustachian tube, if you pushed it any further. While this was an efficient method of keeping the hearing device in place, it subsequently rendered those passengers who successfully managed this feat, completely deaf to the outside world. This made our lives very difficult. Especially when addressing passengers and, in particular, when you were expecting an answer from them. On a full flight, working in the back – that would be economy class – time was of the essence, as we tried to serve a vast amount of people a meal while it was still hot. It was always helpful if, on asking a passenger whether they preferred chicken or beef, they replied promptly with one or the other, so that we could move on to the next row. Pronto. However, on one particular flight, I had to keep repeating my question to a man in a scruffy denim jacket, who was bopping along to the tinny sound emanating from his earphones, which clearly had reached all the way to his inner ear. The passengers on either side of him looked at me sympathetically and said, 'You could say anything to him.' So I shook him by the shoulders, looked into his eyes and mouthed, 'You look like a thief,' to which he replied, 'Beef, please.' On my next trip down the aisle, pushing a trolley laden with tea and coffee pots, I once again patted him on the arm and mouthed, 'Do you need a wee?' He responded, 'Tea, thanks.' If you can't beat them, join them.

Once we were airborne, passengers seated in the smoking section lit up unanimously and, within minutes, the cabin was filled with a smoky haze. There was a very clear line between the non-smoking and smoking sections of the cabin. A significant gap of about ten rows was manned by armed men resembling the Mossad, who patrolled this neutral zone, hauling out anyone who broke the law. Actually it wasn't like that at all. Astonishingly, smoking started in the very next row behind non-smoking. Even worse was that more people wanted to be seated in smoking seats than non-smoking. This made our lives difficult. Believe me, I felt safer having a crack at Oxford Street in the January sales than advising a chain smoker that he was seated in the non-smoking area on a long-haul flight. I risked life and limb once, trying to stop a disgruntled passenger from sneaking into the loo for a quick puff. Determined not to back down, I ordered him to put out his cigarette and threatened him with arrest on landing. When he offered to put his cigarette out in my eyes, I said, 'Oh well, just one little drag, then.' I showed him who was boss.

While the seats in those days were bigger and more comfortable, offering lots of legroom (what's that, I hear you ask), the passenger entertainment system on board was rudimentary. Choice was not an option. Only one movie at a time was shown in each class. People watched the film on a large screen, against the bulkhead of the front row of the cabin. This worked reasonably well for first- and business-class passengers, where there were a limited number of seat rows. But glancing at the screen from the very back row of economy class, one could be forgiven for thinking that Mick Dundee was battling a lizard instead of a crocodile. And heaven forbid you needed to heed a call of nature right in the middle of the picture – there was no pause button. You filled in the gaps yourself.

As soon as the seatbelt lights were switched off, the epic service began. There was no rush. We took our time, as we offered two full rounds of drinks to each and every person. We regarded our passengers as human beings, with hearts and souls, who had paid a lot of money for the privilege of travelling. Most people only dreamt about flying and seeing the world, very few actually experienced it. Flying was a novelty reserved for businessmen, who could afford to travel by air and wealthy families who caught planes to exotic destinations.

Far-fetched as it may sound, we'd been trained to politely allow them time to consider what they would like to drink, to twirl the dinky bottles of a variety of red and white wines between their fingers, perhaps even discuss the merits of the harvest year with a partner, before making their choice. Not once did I roll my eyes heavenwards, tap my manicured fingers on the bar trolley, or sigh deeply as they lingered over this decision. I gave these fare-paying passengers a chance to sip and enjoy their aperitifs, before clearing the tray tables in front of them of debris, to ensure that they had adequate space for the full-size meal tray that was to follow.

Stainless steel cutlery was a luxury that allowed them to cut through fish with a solid knife that didn't bend and deflect the whole tinfoil container of hot food onto the lap of their unsuspecting neighbour. Or even worse, their own. Once again, after dinner, with only our passengers' comfort in mind, we removed the entire tray before offering them a variety of tea, decaffeinated and regular coffee or hot chocolate. We didn't expect them to experience even vague discomfort with a half-eaten meal tray in front of them, fighting for space with a dead gin and tonic, an empty wine bottle, a wine glass and a plastic thimble-full of cold coffee. Passengers were even allowed to use their call bells mid-service, be it only to ask for a drop more milk. Commuters today would never contemplate pushing that button for fear of having their hands chopped off. You might get away with it nowadays, only if it was to report nothing less than a shoe bomber at work in the row in front of you. And even then, you'd have to be really sure about it.

Now you could be pardoned for thinking that this all sounds like something out of a fairy tale. But this is what flying was like in the '80s. Passengers got value for their money. Airlines took pride in earning the title of 'best carrier'. The idea was to make the trip as enjoyable for the passengers as possible, unlike flying today where you are made to feel like a huge inconvenience to a generally surly crew dressed in varying shades of bright orange or lime green. What on earth could inspire the designers of these uniforms to incorporate such a vast amount of orange as to leave the wearers looking like the inside of a cantaloupe melon? And despite what the corporate colours might be, lime green is not a colour that universally flatters everyone who wears it. Just looking at those uniforms could incite me to take up bulimia as a hobby.

We took about three hours to complete the entire service, from drinks to duty-free sales. This left a gap of around five to six hours before the breakfast service, prior to landing at Heathrow. Six hours is a long time to try and stay awake in the dead of night and look glamorous at the same time. Especially on legs that felt as if they had already walked all the way to London.

This is where the 'crew rest' came into play. You may have wondered what that little door, right at the arse end of the plane with 'Crew Only' written on it, was intended for. On some of the planes, there was no door to the crew rest, only a flimsy curtain. Inside were six rock-hard wooden bunks, each with a pillow small enough for a new-born infant to rest half its head on and one scratchy blanket. The duty time was split into two and the crew went to rest in shifts. Now, it was fantastic if you were on the first shift. This meant you got a cool bunk, a fresh scratchy blanket and a starched infant pillow. However, things were not as pleasant for the second shift when the air was stale, the bunk was warm, the blanket dodgy and the pillow completely missing. But, either way, on this first flight of mine, it was heaven to put up my swollen feet. I would have slept on an ironing-board full of maggots.

I didn't find it so hard staying awake for the first shift after dinner. Nor did the passengers. They incessantly rang their bells and popped into the galley asking for drinks, extra blankets and, even a pack of cards. This became tedious. I soon perfected the art of diplomacy, telling them to go to hell in such a way that they thought they'd enjoy the trip there. I almost felt guilty. Only almost. However, the main thing that kept me on my toes was a passenger who kept sneaking into the business-class section, under the hidden cloak of darkness, in search of a comfy seat. The business–class hostie stormed into the galley, where I was sitting on a cold metal bin, inside of which was a rack of still-frozen breakfast meals. She didn't bother with small talk, 'If I catch this passenger of yours trying to sneak into my section one more time, you'll be in trouble.' I didn't have a clue how this was my fault but, still, I approached the man who, by now, had put his economy-class bum back into its originally allocated seat. He had the temerity to look at me suggestively and ask, 'What do you have to do to fly business class?' Nudge nudge, wink wink.

'Earn more money,' I answered. It felt mean, but he deserved it.

The one thing that got me through that flight was when members of the cockpit crew, who were on duty, popped into the galley every so often for a chat. I soon realised that if I thought it was uncomfortable in the small work area, where at least I was able to sit on a hard, cold, metal bin and stretch my legs, it was like lying on a sun-lounger when compared to the close confines of the cockpit, where the pilots and flight engineers sat with their knees in their nostrils. And in a desperate attempt to get blood flowing to my feet, which were tingling with pins and needles, I could at least venture down the aisle. However, passengers would not see this as an opportunity for their revered air hostess to avoid deep-vein thrombosis. No Sirree; they would view this as an opportunity of tugging on my pinafore to ask, 'Excuse me, Miss, could I have …' Give me DVT any day.

Even those pilots and engineers who walked the length of the plane to avoid muscle cramp got suckered into promising cups of tea and coffee. Passengers had no respect for status, or seniority. I especially enjoyed the company of First Officer, Geoff Birchall, with his delightful sense of humour and fondness for practical jokes. Except when I was the victim. He popped into the galley, a smile lighting up his face and enquired how I was coping, as he patted me on the back. What a nice man, I thought. Until, during the breakfast service, a colleague finally pulled the sticky sign off my back which read: 'Crew use only'. Everything is funny, as long as it's happening to someone else.

The long flight finally came to an end. We said goodbye to all our passengers and boarded the bus waiting at the bottom of the steps, after first identifying our Delseys lined up alongside it. We didn't even enter the terminal building; immigration personnel climbed onto the bus at a predetermined stop and checked our ID tags. That's all there was to it. Maybe the English weather was enough of a deterrent back then. Not even an illegal immigrant would voluntarily want to linger in a place this wet.

A girl called Brigitte sat beside me. I'd barely spoken to her during the flight but, on the journey into the city, we got chatting. She asked if I wanted to join her at a football match that evening. Apparently she knew some or other bigwig at 'Man U'. Not only did I not have a clue who 'Man U' were, I was also petrified of attending a football match with all its perceived hooliganism. I had visions of a broken beer bottle being twisted into my face, its jagged edges leaving me with deep wounds that would scar me beyond recognition. No way was I up for that. I'd rather eat an entire hay bale in one sitting. I said yes.

We arrived at the Kensington Palace Hotel, right opposite Kensington Gardens and the magnificent Hyde Park. The hotel was elegant and the location could not have been better. After a shower and two hours of oblivion on a soft mattress, with a deliciously fluffy blanket and a full-sized down pillow, I set out to explore a bit of London in the short time I had available.

It wasn't my first trip to London, I'd been fortunate enough to visit this enchanting city a few times as a child. What struck me this time, after such a long gap, was the abundance of punks and skinheads. Wherever I looked, I saw people my age and younger with pins and studs, leather and chains, kohl-rimmed eyes and black lips. Those who weren't shaved sported multi-coloured Mohicans, like cocks' combs that stuck straight up into the air, gelled into knife-edged sharpness – to be used as self-defence in the event of a headbutt attack, I could only assume.

The city itself had not changed much. Iconic red buses still rushed by, while post boxes, telephone booths and black taxis lined the streets. The Thames still flowed past imposing buildings like the Houses of Parliament, Big Ben and Westminster Abbey, while Tower Bridge watched over the procedures like an elegant, bejewelled old lady. Nelson's Column still stood tall in Trafalgar Square, as millions of people marched by. Crowds lined the Mall in anticipation of the changing of the guards at Buckingham Palace. There never seemed to be a quiet season in London. Oxford Street was always a challenge. I loved the intensity and the buzz of this city, which stretched back to Roman times and attracted people from all around the world.

I still had doubts about this football game I'd agreed to attend. My enthusiasm waned with every step, as I returned to the hotel. I pictured us fighting crowds on busy Tubes and queueing at the stadium for ages for the privilege of sitting on a cold, hard concrete seat, amongst a motley bunch of opposing supporters. In the interest of self-preservation, I made the decision to support the same team as whoever was seated around me favoured.

I had been born with a Fear Of Missing Out. It was an affliction. Somehow, I could never make myself say 'No'. I blamed my mother entirely for passing on these genes. But, in this case, I couldn't figure out what had possessed me to think I'd be missing out on anything if I hadn't accepted an invite to a lousy football game. Turns out I was wrong.

Armed with a pointy umbrella for protection from both the rain and the anticipated violent football thugs, I met Brigitte in the foyer of the hotel. I turned to the door, ready to make our way to the closest Tube station, when she told me that we were being fetched by car. This was a pleasant surprise. It was even more of a pleasant surprise when a silver Bentley pulled up.

I'll never know how Brigitte made the connection, but inside that car were both the chairman and the manager of Manchester United. Not that I would've known either of them if I'd stumbled over them in a floodlit cow patty.

It got better. On arrival at the stadium, a man in a suit ushered us into a private box hosted by none other than the infamous George Best, one of the most colourful footballers of all time. My fear of being stabbed with a broken bottle dissolved as a gin and tonic, in a tall glass, found its way into my willing hand. Brigitte and I hovered on the fringes of this tight-knit football community, but I enjoyed the anonymity of being able to ogle all these celebrities at my leisure. Thank God for FOMO.

I didn't understand, or even pay much attention to the match, but I did know where my loyalties lay. Not with Arsenal.

As an avid tennis player, I had learnt to celebrate a win. On this evening, however, I was surprised to discover that we were about to celebrate not losing. But that didn't mean our team (I was by now a committed 'Man U' supporter) had won, either. The match was a draw, which appeared to have been a better result than expected. This led to further celebrations in Mayfair, at George Best's club called 'Blondes'. After copious quantities of pink champagne, Brigitte and I finally found ourselves back at the Kensington Palace Hotel at 5.30 a.m..

London became one of my favourite destinations, to the extent that I typically requested a London flight once a month. Needless to say, I passed a lot of strawberry champagne and Lindt chocolates across that counter at the roster office. I couldn't bear to be parted from this distinguished city for too long. I inhaled the vibrant atmosphere as I got to know it, mostly on foot, exploring every inch, visiting every landmark and attending every theatre production. If I could have, I would've saved the air of London in a bottle.

Perhaps this enigmatic city holds a special place in my heart, because it was the venue for my first carnal encounter with an aviator. It was the greying sideburns that did it. And the lack of a wedding band. And possibly the four, broad, gold bands on the uniform sleeve. Or maybe it was just due to lack of competition. It all began when I went to introduce myself to the cockpit crew at the start of the journey in Johannesburg. I said hello to the co-pilot, the boy pilot and the flight engineers. Oddly, the captain was sitting on the jump seat. The tiny cabin was positively swarming with testosterone. So many men in such a tiny cubicle could not be healthy, especially when the Oxford dictionary defines a cockpit as 'a place where a contest is fought or which has been the scene of many contests or battles'. They may as well have added 'over air hostesses'. However, they all seemed like perfectly nice guys, but not a looker between them. In fact, two of them had such large Adam's apples that together they could have yielded an entire vat of cider. Looking at them, I resigned myself to the fact that Lizzy and I would be doing our own thing in London during our layover.

I was working upstairs in the SUD and therefore had the 'privilege' of serving the cockpit. I busied myself preparing their hot drinks and was about to pick up the tray and make my way back to the pointy end of the plane, when Kevin Costner stepped into the galley. It wasn't really Kev, but a very good replica of him. My knees threatened to abandon all pretence of support as I looked into that handsome face. My insides felt like the congealed custard in a week-old trifle. He still had a cap on his head and I couldn't miss the four gold bars, as he lifted his arm up to remove it. He told me his name was Dieter and then held my hand in both of his as he said, 'That's a lovely name. German, is it?' 'Well, yes. But I wasn't born there. My father's German, but he wasn't born there, either. Actually, I don't even think his parents were born there. And my mother's from Ireland, or at least her ancestors are, so I'm not sure why they chose a German name for me. And it means little Margaret.' Oh Jesus, should I shoot myself now, or wait for the verbal haemorrhage to stop first? Then it hit me – maybe he was referring to his own name?

'Anyway, what are you doing here? The captain's already on board,' I asked, still cringing after the flood of nervous drivel that had spewed from the gaping wound that was my mouth.

'Bob's the JACOB. I'm in command.' Not arrogant, just putting things into perspective. JACOB stood for 'just another captain on board', an acronym not hugely favoured by the men in question – not so much of the 'just another'. They felt COB had a more commanding ring to it. Hmmm … two captains, one aeroplane. Didn't bode well.

But then, I noticed that Dieter was as charming towards his male colleagues as he was to the opposite sex. He had the knack of making everyone feel special. But I did get the impression that he put in a bit more effort with me. I loved the way he used my name frequently. Maybe it was because the moniker rolled off his Teutonic tongue with the ease of a native speaker. The chemistry between us was tangible. It's probably the best service they ever had, as I constantly popped into the cockpit to offer drinks, snacks, newspapers, even an emery board and refreshing eye gel.

This must have been the first time ever that I felt disappointed when the flight finally came to an end. It was probably also the first time that any passenger in my section had ever felt that, too. Normally, I got the feeling that they couldn't wait to put as much distance as possible between themselves and me, as they sprung up out of their seats before the engines had even shut down, grabbed their bags from the overhead lockers and scuttled off the plane. My positive attitude had extended to them as well. Nothing had been too much effort for me – I would've bathed their feet in Epsom salts as I strolled up and down the aisle, searching for someone – anyone – who needed attention, a beatific smile no doubt spread across my face.

We identified our luggage and lined up to board the crew bus. Lizzy's bag was still hiding somewhere in the intestines of the aircraft, so I boarded the bus, took a seat and kept the one next to me free for her. Ostensibly.

Imagine my elation when Dieter climbed the stairs, glanced around and then placed his fully clad rear end firmly in the seat next to me. He didn't even ask if it was free, such was his confidence in the matter of our mutual admiration. Loyalty flew out the window as Lizzy stepped into the bus and looked at me, a frown forming an amused exclamation mark between her eyebrows. Despite the derisive sniggers from the back of the bus, where the less masculine stewards gathered and the whispered words, 'cockpit fly', drifted over my head, I was happier than I'd ever been.

We flirted for the entire duration of the bus journey, aware of the eavesdropping ears of the rest of the crew, which called for a measure of discretion. They didn't witness the pressure of his thigh as it pushed against mine, though. Ha! As we approached Marble Arch, I still wasn't quite sure how this was going to end as, sadly, we were about to be dropped off at our hotel in Kensington. The cockpit crew resided in the much more lavish Portman Hotel in Marylebone. Then it came … the words I'd been waiting for … 'Would you like …' 'Yes!' I replied. '… to meet up for dinner tonight?' A girl should never appear too keen. 'Seven. Your foyer.'

Seven o'clock. My foyer. An appallingly dressed man was staring intently at the prints on the wall above the receptionist's head. I noticed the fake Polo shirt from Hong Kong, pants that hovered ever so slightly above the ankles and scuffed shoes that were old enough to vote. He was the same height as the captain on my flight. He had the same greying sideburns as my captain. Same square shoulders. When he turned around, at least the gorgeous face was untarnished by civilian clothes. My heart lurched with lust. Not bad. From the waist up. I'd get over the lack of fashion sense. It wasn't a major problem – I could always buy his clothes for him; teach him a bit of style. He clearly didn't spend money on himself. I had always admired people who didn't have a passion for all things material. I did, however, notice the watch. Genuine. Not from some side alley in Kowloon. If there are two things a pilot will spend money on, it's his watch and his aviator sunglasses. I'm not sure which came first, Ray Bans or pilots.

He took my arm and linked it through his, as we stepped out onto the street. Exactly how I had always pictured it in my dreams. The next part in my reverie was where he hailed a black cab and whipped me off to some intimate restaurant in the heart of Mayfair to be wined and dined, followed by cheek-to-cheek dancing in a dimly lit nightclub.

Maybe he was saving that for the next time. But, for now, he suggested we step into the Spaghetti House at end of the road, barely a 100 yards from my hotel. Oh-kay. Who cared if I was overdressed? Nothing mattered in the bloom of love.

Decades later I still ask myself, 'What is it about missing signals in the toxic flush of endorphins?' But back then, I couldn't have spotted cheap from the inside of a bargain store.

I liked to think of myself as a modern woman, but when he asked for separate bills at the end of our meal, I just about choked on the cockroach in my cappuccino. Even the waiter looked shocked. Was he stingy? Stingy??!! He was tighter than a nun's nunu. At this point, my libido was beginning to hit a downward spiral. His attraction was dwindling as rapidly as my meal allowance on a shopping spree.

He must've noticed my waning enthusiasm and suggested we walk through Hyde Park, in order to rekindle the romantic ambience that had existed prior to my having had to run back to the hotel to fetch my purse, so that I could pay for my half of the meal, notwithstanding the fact that he had consumed both a starter and dessert, in addition to a main course.

The late summer dusk light of the park did, indeed, work its magic and I soon forgot about the uncomfortable financial interlude of earlier, as he kissed me rather enthusiastically under the proverbial streetlamp. Batting his wandering hands away, I felt it was time to head back to my hotel before we were arrested for public indecency.

We barely made it to the room when the parted teeth of his zip gave way and his too-short trousers fell to his ankles. Old-fashioned briefs stared back at me. The kind called underpants and that even my father had finally eschewed when I was just a baby. It dawned on me that he might well be as old as my father. As he stood naked in front of me, I realised that he was nowhere near as physically toned in the flesh as I thought he had been in his full uniform. His pubic hairs matched his sideburns. In colour, not texture. Paper-thin skin hung in creased little folds from his buttocks, like a perfectly ironed pleated skirt. This was all very disappointing. But then again, I guess I didn't look exactly like Bo Derek myself after an entire bowl of spaghetti carbonara.

To say that things were awkward, is to put it mildly. Sure, I'd fantasised about romancing a pilot since joining the airline, but even I had basic requirements. And although I'd never been promiscuous, I was experienced enough to know that Dieter was not the most competent lover a girl could ever have. Maybe I would have to look further than the silver sideburns in future.

No sooner were the sexual gymnastics concluded, when he sat up, or rather, leant seductively on one elbow, as the soft flesh hung like a roman blind from his upper arm, and dropped a bombshell. It was so unexpected, jarring and utterly out of line. Had he said, 'I'm married,' or, 'I'm a serial killer,' or even, 'I have to tell you that I once drove over the postman with a forklift,' I would not have been more surprised. The words that came out of his presumptuous mouth were something along the lines of, 'You're very nice and I enjoy your company (and the fact that you don't complain about paying for yourself), but I've just come out of a long-term relationship and I'm not looking for anything serious right now.'

The horror I felt was worse than if I'd been caught behind the bicycle shed giving the bishop a blow-job. 'Relationship?' I yelled. 'What gives you the right to lie in my bed, more loose skin on one arm than on an entire Shar Pei puppy, and treat me like a needy, loveless single woman desperately searching for commitment?' Of course I didn't say any of that. I meekly answered, 'Me neither,' as he got up and pulled on his old-fashioned briefs and short trousers before kissing me on the forehead – *the forehead?* – and disappearing out of the door, into the long passage, like an undercover agent. Watching him slink away I couldn't help thinking that his mother would have done the world a favour if she had thrown him away and rather kept the stork.

So that was my first real encounter with a pilot. But I'm all for denial. The next day I managed to convince not only Lizzy, but also myself that I had never really fancied him at all. Even in his uniform. That kept me happy as a sandboy, as long as my best friend kept up her promise to swap working positions with me on the flight home.

Another good reason to visit London in the summer was Wimbledon. Having an ex-professional tennis player in the family had its benefits. We always managed to get tickets, which not only gave us entry to this world-famous event, but allowed us access to the players' lounges. In the '80s, relaxed security in that area meant literally rubbing shoulders with the likes of Jimmy Connors, Boris Becker, Chris Evert, Martina Navratilova and many others. I went back year after year, but they never recognised me.

Abortion was legal in London from the very early years. Abortion was only legalised in South Africa in 1996 and, even today poverty, lack of access to information and stigma still remain significant barriers to safe abortion. So, when a friend of mine, Nerina, asked me to request a London flight with her in the beginning days of our flying careers, I thought no more of it, assuming she simply needed a shopping and sight-seeing partner. On the flight over, nothing seemed to be out of the ordinary but, once we got to our hotel in London, she was loath to commit to meeting up at all. I found that quite odd but, as I didn't know her particularly well, I assumed that perhaps she was a moody person and had changed her mind about me being her new best friend. It didn't bother me too much – I was quite happy strolling around London on my own and wasn't in the least concerned about sitting down to a meal in a sidewalk café alone.

The following morning I tried to ring Nerina, but got no answer from her room. I assumed she had definitely changed her mind about our friendship. Hey, I was no stranger to rejection so, once again, I entertained myself in the coffee shops on Oxford Street. I did begin to wonder why she had wanted me to do the flight with her, though. We had ended up on one or two flights together before and had always got on very well, but had never pursued an active friendship outside of the airline. Later that day, I slid a note under her door just to ask if she was okay, as I'd not been able to get hold of her. This brought no response, either.

The following afternoon, when it was time to board the bus to the airport, she appeared in the hotel foyer looking diffident and wan. In fact, she looked awful. But when I asked her if she was alright, she convinced me that all was well. It was only on the return flight that night, as we sat side by side on cold, metal bins in the galley, that she confided in me. She had come to London to have an abortion, but had to do it on a working flight so that neither her parents, nor her boyfriend, would ever suspect. My heart went out to her and I could not forgive myself for having been so callous as to have allowed her to go through that terrible emotional and physical ordeal on her own. If only I had been more persistent. She left the airline soon after that and I lost touch with her altogether.

With so many flights in and out of London, it was inevitable that occasionally things went wrong. On one particular flight, shortly after take-off from Heathrow, the pilots identified a problem which required us to return to base. We had to dump fuel as soon as possible. They radioed in to request permission from the control tower, 'This is Springbok 236. Request permission to dump fuel and return to base. Over.'

Unfortunately, at this point, the plane found itself directly over Windsor Castle. The air traffic controller felt obliged to deny the request, 'Permission denied. The Queen is currently in residence.'

The pilot wasted no time, 'Ask the lady if she would like just the fuel, or if she would prefer the whole damn plane.'

'Permission granted. Over.'

5

FORAY INTO THE FAR EAST

My fascination with the exotic Far East was about to become a reality. Hong Kong and Taipei were next on my agenda. But, included in these slippings was a night on the enchanting island of Mauritius, on the outbound leg. I couldn't have planned a better vacation myself.

My first recollection of this volcanic island in the Indian Ocean was not one of beaches, lagoons and coral reefs; it was one of gratitude for having survived the road trip from the unpronounceable Sir Seewoosagur Ramgoolam International Airport to our hotel at the south-western tip of the island. I'm being generous referring to these single-lane, potholed tracks as roads. And I would be pushing artistic licence to the nth degree by calling the vehicles that wove haphazardly along these tracks, avoiding both dogs and potholes, roadworthy cars. We lurched around corners, slammed on brakes, dodged head-on collisions and, at times, I could swear, we even took to the air in a fashion reminiscent of Chitty Chitty Bang Bang.

To call the journey hair-raising would be an understatement. It was body-numbingly, brain-tinglingly petrifying. And yet, I always knew we would reach our destination in the end. What is it about travelling in foreign countries that leads to delusions of being invincible?

By the time the coach pulled up at the luxurious Meridien Paradis Hotel, my heartbeat had slowed down to a blur. Finally, I was able to take in the beauty of Mauritius in the late afternoon light. It was exquisite. And just for the record, however he said it, Mark Twain was right: 'Mauritius was made first and then heaven, heaven being copied after Mauritius.' Not that I'd seen heaven yet, I'd just come very close to it in the past half-hour.

To call the water turquoise is to do it an injustice. Opaque and transparent, it laps at snow-white beaches. Causarina trees border grassy banks at the edge of the sand. A barrier of coral reef gives rise to a natural lagoon, safe from sharks and breaking waves. The water is still and crystal clear. To me it was heart-stoppingly beautiful the first time I saw it, and it still has the same effect on me today.

Mauritius was originally 'discovered' by a Portuguese navigator, was then occupied successively by the Dutch and the French, and finally ceded to Great Britain, before its independence in 1968. The multi-ethnic society is made up of people of Indian, African, European and Chinese origin. Their delightful Creole lilt, as they repeat the sing-song motto of life on the island 'No problem in Mauritius', endears them to everyone who visits it.

Our hotel was situated right on the beach, with the swimming pool as a focal point. The bar, with its bandstand, was at one end and sea sand at the other. We drank and dined and then danced under a canopy of stars. For the entire period of my flying career, the only bands I ever heard in Mauritius were Lionel Ritchie impersonators. Well-suited to the romance of the island and certainly a catalyst for my 'almost' second fling with an airman, as well. It should never have happened. I blame it entirely on the Pina Coladas. And Lionel Richie. Brendon held me close as we danced. In hindsight, I think the only reason he held me so close was to keep himself upright. But at the time, I didn't care. He was terribly attractive. As the band started packing up, I whispered to him, 'Would you like to ... er ... can I ... offer you a nightcap in my room?'

To which he replied, 'When? Like now, you mean?'

'No,' I said, 'I was thinking more like next Christmas.' My humour had an arousing effect on him. He lunged towards me and, as I playfully avoided him and headed towards my room, he lurched behind me like a lopsided Land Rover on a potholed track. After a little trouble getting my key into the lock, we fell inside the room and promptly fell upon each other. Suddenly he sat up, clutched his head in his hands and said, 'No. No. Oh fug, fug, Chrisd'

'What?' I asked, alarmed.

'Noooo,' he wailed. By now he looked so agitated that I thought he might be suffering acute myocardial infarction.

I tugged at his arms and legs, as I started placing him in the recovery position. 'What is it?'

'I carnd. Carnd do this.'

'Is it your heart?' I asked. My own heart was pounding. I wondered if I should leave him and go and look for a security guard to help me drag him to Reception, from where they could call an ambulance.

'Yesh. I'm in love with you. But jush remmmembered, I already have wife.'

We both laughed so much that I forgot to feel humiliated, as he staggered off in search of his own room.

I spent the following morning prostrate on a silver beach, where I happily succumbed to the soporific effects of the sun. Fruit sellers, balancing baskets of fat litchis and mangoes, criss-crossed the hot sand, their voices with seductive French accents calling out to advertise their wares. Others offered fresh pineapples, which they peeled to resemble an ice cream cone. In the background, men on boats solicited business, offering day trips to 'Coconut Island' and other exotic locations. I was tempted. Time, unfortunately, didn't permit.

All too soon, I had to return to my room to prepare for the hazardous journey back to the airport. If it wasn't for the allure of the next destination, I might have dug in my heels, both out of fear of the road trip and an overwhelming desire to spend the rest of my days in this utopia.

As the time before, the bus trip was terrifying and hot. And, also as the time before, the gods concurred and delivered us safely to the aircraft. Invincible, as always.

It was a funny thing that no matter how lethargic one felt, or what time of the morning or night it was, the minute we stepped on board, ebullience kicked in. We moved with fervour; everyone pulled their weight as we prepped the plane, amidst chatter and laughter. In this instance, I would probably have gone as far as to kiss the passengers' feet as they stepped on board, so grateful was I to have been able to spend twenty-four hours on this magical atoll.

Except, this time, I didn't have to; they were already on board. The flight had originated in Johannesburg, it was just the crew who got off in Mauritius, while the passengers remained in their seats for the entire journey through to Hong Kong.

Overseas flights were generally filled to maximum capacity. Hong Kong was no exception. Unlike my previous flights, though, I immediately realised that communication was going to be a problem here. Most of the passengers were Chinese. Hardly any of them spoke English and not a single crew member spoke Mandarin or Cantonese. We had a tough ten hours to look forward to. In hindsight, I'd rather have knelt on a bag of frozen peas for the entire ten hours than try and smile through the service. It was hard for these passengers to express what they wanted. And frustrating for all of us. I was offended at the way they spoke to me, feeling as if I was being berated by their constant intonation. In retaliation, I raised my voice, hoping that speaking louder would lead to understanding. We tacitly agreed that they would stop interrupting me, while I was ignoring them. They smiled and nodded to let me know that they respected me and the way in which I had sorted out the situation.

I was used to being called many things during my flying career – hostie, trolley dolly, waitress, 'skews me', Miss, and in the latter years, it progressed to cabin attendant. The only difference between a hostie and a cabin attendant is about 10kg. Passengers generally thought we were there purely to provide them with endless cups of tea and coffee, and to replenish their whiskeys during the entire flight. They had no idea just how versatile we were. We dealt with deaths on board, births on board, fires on board, stowaways on board and pilots off-board. The latter being the most challenging. But, in all seriousness, our main function on board was as a safety official. Just as pilots were often referred to as glorified bus drivers, which was all fine and dandy until things went wrong. You wouldn't want a bus driver attempting to land a jumbo jet, on an unlit runway, with one engine and no nose wheel. That's why buses don't have wings.

Our second most important function, apart from acting as scantily qualified paramedics, was one of PR. It's no secret that it is cabin crew who sell an airline. People judge airlines purely based on their experiences in the air. The public never check that all the latest technical records and service history of the aircraft are up to date and, no matter how much the check-in staff on the ground piss passengers off, they get over that in no time at all, with the anticipated glee of relaxing in a seat with a 'skews me' serving them drinks for fourteen solid hours. Speaking from experience, when I was in a good mood, happy with life, my patience with passengers knew no bounds. But let me have been called out on standby for a flight that was taking me somewhere I particularly did not want to go, at a particular time and for a particular reason, I had the ability to make passengers wish they had chosen to fly on a broomstick with a defective avionics compartment instead. There is one specific passenger I recall who would never want to fly on SAA again, but that was entirely self-inflicted.

Barry, Lizzy and I had done our utmost to cajole an obnoxious man who, while he wasn't doing anything actually *verboten*, was being extremely annoying – for instance, stretching his legs out into the aisle for us to trip over, despite numerous requests for him to remove said legs from aisle. Before take-off already he had irritated me, as he interrupted the safety demonstration by continually asking for a drink. Lizzy suggested ramming the trolley into his shins. He must've overheard her because, as I came careering down the aisle on my way to hand out headsets, he jerked his feet out of the way just as I skimmed his armrest. I smiled at him. He didn't smile back. Throughout the flight he kept ringing his call bell, requesting that the cabin either be cooled down, or heated up, or he needed another blanket. It was endless. Then Barry came up with an idea. I didn't realise then that it was not actually his idea at all – it was a tactic employed by many airline crew around the world. An effective treatment for exactly this kind of behaviour.

Lizzy went to have a word with the captain. He didn't even ask to hear the passenger's side of the story. We looked up his name on the gen dec. The captain radioed ahead and advised the customs officials that we had a passenger on board who was behaving in a suspicious manner, and hinted that he thought the man might be carrying illegal substances or some other form of contraband. After landing, on the crew bus with a celebratory drink in our hands, we toasted him and sincerely hoped that he'd enjoyed having an internal cavity search with a rubber glove. We never saw him on South African Airways again.

Eventually, we took to the skies and the service got under way. The glamour of the job disappeared as I got pushed, grabbed, prodded, tugged at and coughed on, until I almost had suicidal thoughts. Trying to manage a dinner service, on a full plane, with many requests for 'special meals' – vegetarian, seafood, children's – had its challenges. I have to confess, I did notice the illuminated call light overhead one passenger which I ignored, as I was in the middle of handing out about 3 million little trays with foil-covered meals. Every single other crew member was also ignoring the fact that this passenger had clearly pushed the button with the picture of an air hostess on it.

Finally, once everyone had a tray in front of them, the crew gathered in the galley, prepping for the next part of the service. We had all forgotten about our passenger with the call light on. Suddenly, an agitated little man stormed into the galley, and in his best attempt at English, said, 'I been 'fingeling' hostess ten minutes now and still she not come!' Needless to say, the humour was lost on him.

The flight finally came to an end. As this was my first visit to Hong Kong, the captain invited me to sit on a jump seat in the cockpit for the spectacular approach.

Kai Tak airport was located on the west side of Kowloon Bay in Kowloon. I could not believe that we were going to try and negotiate a landing here. We appeared to be surrounded by rugged mountains. Every direction I looked in, I saw a range of hills that all looked tall, very tall. And then there was the harbour ...

At the one end of the runway, buildings rose up to six stories just across the road. The other three sides of the runway were surrounded by Victoria Harbour. I strained against my seatbelt for a better view out of the cockpit window, throughout this low-altitude manoeuvre, as the pilots were required to line the plane up with the runway. During this final approach, we practically passed between ladies hanging up their washing. I am pretty sure I even glimpsed the flickering of a television screen through an apartment window. The massive aircraft continued moving, as if with no regard for this densely populated area and crowded harbour. I had always been led to believe that airports were built outside of the city for safety and pollution reasons. Not in Hong Kong.

I didn't utter a word as we reached a small hill, on which I spotted a huge orange-and-white checkerboard. This board was used as a visual reference point for the final approach. I made a promise to God that if He allowed me to survive this landing, I would be nice to every single passenger in the future. And I would learn Mandarin.

The runway loomed below and in front of us like a hologram. We seemed to be about to touchdown, just feet off the ground, when the plane turned again. Both of the pilots' and the flight engineer's faces were creased in concentration. They had screwed up and missed the opportunity to land this Jumbo Jet. We were about to hit the deck in the most spectacular fashion. I wondered if I should warn them. I didn't. This was a classic case of, 'I'd rather die than make a fool of myself'.

It was only after landing that I learned that this world-famous manoeuvre was widely known in the piloting community as the 'Hong Kong turn' or 'checkerboard turn'. Amongst passengers, it became known as the 'Kai Tak heart attack' which resonated with me. I totally understood why it was regarded at the sixth most dangerous airport in the world and was ecstatic to have survived my inaugural landing there. Now all I had to do was make good on my promise to be nice to all my passengers in future. Oh ... and learn Mandarin.

Kai Tak was initially located far away from residential areas, but the expansion of both residential districts and the airport resulted in this airport becoming much closer to the densely populated areas. For this reason, there was a restriction on the height of buildings that could be built in Kowloon. There was also serious noise pollution for nearby residents, resulting in a night curfew from midnight to 6.30 a.m. for aircraft take-offs and landings.

Landing at this airport was technically demanding for pilots, but clearly also dramatic to experience from a passenger's perspective. I thanked Jesus, Mary and Joseph that we were not trying to land in the middle of a typhoon, with strong and gusty crosswinds. This would have been a challenge I could do without! I could just imagine it from a spectator's point of view — watching these large aircraft banking at low altitudes must have been beyond thrilling.

There were many incidents and accidents over the years at this perilous, but magnificent airport. These included hitting the approach lights of the runway while landing in rain and fog, which eventually culminated in the aircraft running off the tarmac and slipping into the harbour. On another occasion an aircraft overran the runway, while landing during a typhoon. It touched down more than two-thirds along the strip and was unable to stop before it ran out of taxiway. Although the aircraft ended up submerged beyond the end of the airstrip, there were only twenty-three minor injuries amongst the 396 passengers and crew on board. This gave me confidence to continue returning to this exotic destination.

Eventually, for all these reasons, the government decided to build a new commercial airport on the island of Chek Lap Kok, off Lantau Island. I suspect they grew tired of fishing aeroplanes out of the water.

Nothing looked familiar to me during the transfer from the airport to our hotel. It was like setting foot on a different planet. The road signs, consisting of bright-red Asian characters, looked alien. Instead of metal rods, the scaffolding around huge building developments was made out of bamboo. I saw a sea of people in every direction I looked — like an army of ants permanently on the march. A myriad cars filled every space on the road, with barely a gap for pedestrians to pass. The vibrancy of it all filled me with excitement; I couldn't wait to get out and meet this city. It was a pity that, in time, my senses would become blunted to this unique wonder that I experienced on my first visit to the Far East.

We finally arrived at the five-star Harbour View Holiday Inn on Kowloon. The location couldn't have been better; it was situated right on the water. The staff fell over themselves to welcome us. I could force myself to get used to this. We were allocated rooms for the duration of our stay and simultaneously handed an envelope containing a very generous meal allowance, as well as a subsistence and travel allowance. I was delighted – this seemed an extremely fortuitous arrangement: to leave behind a lonely one-bedroom flat in exchange for a luxury hotel, with built-in entertainment around the clock. In the queue in front of me, the co-pilot opened his envelope and, overjoyed at the sight of such an extravagant amount of Hong Kong dollars bulging out of it, announced, 'I shall spend some of this on booze, some on women and the rest foolishly!' That just about sums up the attitude of the entire cockpit crew.

Despite the long flight and the hectic time change, it was an expectation that we would all gather in the captain's room for a 'de-briefing', once we'd had a quick shower and changed our clothes. By now, I was well-versed in airline practice, so I had brought my own little miniature bottle of gin and a can of tonic off the plane for this purpose, regardless of the fact that it was only about eight in the morning, local time. The reasoning behind it was that we had worked all through the night, thereby missing our usual little evening tipple, in which other mortals would ordinarily have been partaking. I didn't need much convincing.

They say that four out of five people suffer from jet lag. Does that mean that one out of five enjoys it? Jet lag is a strange sensation. It's a cross between feeling as if you've been poked awake with an electric cattle prod and being hungover. Sometimes on waking up, I wondered if I was still inebriated. It took some getting used to. I would wake up in a dark room that looked familiar – but in the end, all hotel rooms looked the same. On waking, the only way of knowing where I was, was to open the curtains and see which skyline I was presented with. Ah, the Eiffel Tower – I must be in Paris. Statue of Liberty – forgot that I'd actually bid for a New York flight. Perth – again. And so it went. People always asked how I coped with jet lag. On outbound flights, it was easier. Arriving in a luxury hotel room, with no answer-phone messages to listen to, no washing to sort out, no shopping to unpack and no-one to ring, I simply removed my make-up, had a shower, unpacked, drew the thick blackout blinds and went to sleep for two or three hours, with absolutely no risk of the disturbances associated with daily life. Well, that's how it should have been. But for some reason, no matter where I travelled, on the day of my arrival, the very minute that I slid my exhausted body between those cool, starched sheets and slipped into a deep, dreamless sleep – the kind that is described as an especially refreshing part of the sleep cycle, unless you are awakened out of it, in which case you will feel very sluggish and experience 'sleep drunkenness', during which it is unsafe to drive – the fire alarm would go off, loud enough to wake the dead, indicating a fire drill. During deep sleep, all energy goes into recharging your batteries: your kidneys clean your blood, your organs detox (or try to), cells are replaced (in my case, only fat cells), muscle tissue builds up (don't fall for that one) and memories are consolidated (the ones you try so hard to obliterate). I lay the blame squarely at the foot of fire drills in hotels all around the world for the fact that my blood, organs, cells, muscle tissue and memory have never developed to their full potential.

On returning home after flights, it was impossible to toss everything aside and climb into bed, no matter how upset my circadian rhythms might have been. It was all my brain's fault. It kept yelling, 'I know it's light outside. You can't trick me.' The best cure was exercise. And a relatively early night. Well, that was always the intention.

Fatigue, hunger and jet lag affect one's judgement. I was always tired, hungry and jet-lagged and therefore take no responsibility for the fact that I accepted the offer of an engagement ring from some dear, lovely man a few years into my flying career. It was difficult being in a relationship with an earthling. Flying around the world, spending most of my time away from home, required a very understanding partner. He also needed to be able to accept me returning home jetlagged and sick and tired of smiling, being convivial, affable and polite, wanting only to be left alone. On arrival home, I'd say, 'Hello, my darling. Awful trip. I love and adore you and I've missed you. Honest.' What I really wanted to say, in the nicest possible way, of course, was, 'But I'm tired. Now will you please bugger off and leave me alone.' Then thankfully, two days later I'd be packing for my next trip. Needless to say, he was neither understanding nor accepting. I refused to stop flying. He asked for his ring back. We both lived happily ever after.

On my first night in Hong Kong, I felt as if I'd been dumped headlong into a fairy tale. Gazillions of lights lit up the highest point and occasionally even the entire outline of a building. They had to be static, as a flickering light could be confused with those indicating starboard and portside on an aircraft. Not, as I thought, out of consideration for those poor souls afflicted by migraines or epilepsy, where flashing lights could trigger an attack. Ambling along the walkways alongside Hong

Kong harbour, was magical. Even the hardest heart should find romance hidden in the twinkling glow. The reflections shimmered in the water, like the fizz from a champagne bottle as the cork is popped. If ever anyone thought about falling in love, this would be the place to do it.

The toilets in Hong Kong, however, presented a slightly less romantic element to the uninitiated. In fact, *they* might have had the ability to induce the unprovoked onset of migraine or epilepsy, if the lights didn't. While all was hunky-dory and very much to my liking in the luxurious hotels we were accustomed to, public ablutions were to be avoided at all cost. Only an extreme emergency could force you into one of these little girl's rooms. The same was true of the latrines at local restaurants. People always enquired snarkily why air hostesses had such strong thigh muscles. Now, there might have been a number of contributing factors to this unique phenomenon, but one of them certainly was due to the fact that we had to squat dangerously over gaping holes in the ground in order to relieve ourselves of the pressure of liquid in the bladder. However, even at the prospect of blowing up like the ill-fated Challenger, no female crew member would ever attempt to seek relief from a number two in a Hong-Kongese-type toilet. Imagine an old Victorian bathhouse, dank and musty, with pools of water coagulating on the floors. Now close your eyes and imagine it again, only a hundred times worse. Personal hygiene, in this British protectorate, was not conducted with the same rigour as in the West. Health standards were definitely below par. Between the street food and lack of sanitation, dysentery, hepatitis and stomach parasites were a very real possibility. Unfortunately, the two were closely linked – after the food came the urge. And then the purge.

The lavatories generally all resembled one another, but there were slight variations. I recall once walking into a damp concrete room, consisting of a line of individual little cubicles, with about two rows of bricks on either side, to shield you from prying eyes. Only this time, there was no squat hole, just a narrow furrow running through the centre of the cubicle. Water flowed down this little channel at a slight angle from the facilities at the top end of the room. Perhaps I'm being generous referring to it as water. It was an opaque combination of seawater and urine. The odour was horrendous. There were two painted footprints on either side of this groove, indicating that I had to squat with one leg each side, thereby precariously placing my private parts closer to this dike – which I feared was in peril of bursting its banks and flooding my newly purchased Reeboks – than I wished to. But, further up the line from me was clearly a local inhabitant of the island who had no perception of either shame or guilt, since I watched a big, brown lump of excrement make its way between my legs. I stared in horror as my stream of urine bounced back off this submarine and splashed onto … my newly purchased Reeboks. Okay, so Confucius might have said, 'Size of man's poo direct indication of his wealth,' but give me poverty any day.

Hong Kong was a kaleidoscope of colour and a maelstrom of chaos, an unavoidable consequence of more than 5 million people living in close proximity. The Star Ferry could be counted on to carry full loads of commuters across the bay between Hong Kong and the Kowloon Peninsula. Old-fashioned junks snaked between the water traffic, sails billowing, like painted pictures. Aged, wiry men, with barely an ounce of flesh covering their bones, pulled rickshaws in the streets. Their toothless grins bore testimony to the perils of the traffic, as they artfully dodged trucks, cars, tuk-tuks and scooters carrying entire families. Horns buzzed and engines revved. Street vendors everywhere tempted cast-iron stomachs with aromas of garlic, peanut oil, fried pork or chicken, pak choi and a plethora of other enticing flavours and fragrances. Men and women walked along the streets holding wicker birdcages aloft, many of them empty but some housing a variety of small, winged creatures. Yet others clutched clear plastic bags filled with locusts. Animated shouts punctured the air in side streets and dilapidated buildings. I'd never even heard of mah-jong before.

I was innocently walking down the street when I was pulled behind a cluster of cardboard boxes by a man so excited he was frothing at the mouth. I almost fainted; my heart banged in my chest. Fear went all the way through to my internal organs. Little bits of spittle hit my face, as he babbled incoherently and thrust a stash of fake Rolexes under my nose. At first, I wasn't sure if he was selling them, or if he was asking me to hide them under my top as he beat a hasty retreat from the police. Cowardice claimed victory and I turned and ran. By the time I'd reached the end of the block, I realised that there was no threat; this was simply the preferred sales technique of overzealous salesmen. The same thing happened every few metres. To this day, I'm still sitting with a jewellery box filled to bursting with one-dollar watches.

Further down the road, a vendor was pushing a barrel. The short, bandy-legged man took one scathing glance at my horrifically bright pink Lacoste shirt and gesticulated (i.e. in English, threw a tantrum) that it was a poor copy, whereas his were the real thing. He may as well have prodded me in the ribs with a stick. I felt like pointing out to him that his shop was kind of a dump and his sales etiquette needed work, but we didn't have the conversation. Call me gullible or intimidated; I bought three more.

As a keen dressmaker, I found Wing On Street, or 'Cloth Alley' as it was better known to Westerners, enchanting with its richly coloured swirls of fabric. Shopping was a delight, as Hong Kong provided a multitude of markets that swallowed up most of our meal allowance – the Night Market, Temple Street Market, Mon Kok Market, to name a few. Stanley Market was an all-day ordeal that involved a journey on the Number 6 bus, which chugged its way over the mountainous terrain to Stanley Bay. Clothing was cheap, but small. Foodstuff proved less popular with the crew. Glazed, pressed ducks dangled in windows. Dried seafood and fruit and vegetables in barrels lined the streets. We didn't recognise most of it. Michael, a gay steward with the most reprehensible sense of humour, pointed at a wheelbarrow containing what he thought resembled dried up scrotum. He then hauled out his wallet and, entirely for our benefit, asked the Chinese vendor for 'a baker's dozen of scroti, please'.

This very same steward, Michael, had me incontinent with laughter a few years later on a London layover. He had been feeling rather ill on the flight over and asked me to accompany him to the pharmacy down the road from the hotel on arrival. In his pocket, he had a prescription from his doctor at home for suppositories. I never knew what condition he was suffering from, or why he carried that prescription with him, but clearly it wasn't serious as he remains in good health today, no doubt still entertaining people with his wit. We joined the queue and finally the man in his white coat enquired what he could do for us. Michael handed him the prescription. A couple of minutes later the pharmacist returned, handed over a packet of medication and enquired whether he had used suppositories before. To which Michael mischievously replied, 'No.' The chemist then began the rather sensitive task of explaining to Michael that they were to be inserted rectally and not ingested orally. Michael pretended to be horrified at this. 'And,' the pharmacist added, 'they must be taken with food.'

'With food?' Michael questioned. 'Well, then, I'd better get a sandwich.' He then appeared all flustered and asked the man, 'So, sorry to have to ask you this, but do I push the sandwich up first and then the pill, or do I first push the pill up and follow it with the sandwich?' I snorted in a very unladylike manner. The poor pharmacist wasn't sure how to behave – all British stiff upper lip to the fore. He couldn't figure out if Michael was having him on. I could see him trying to keep his composure and maintain a professional attitude as he continued to give coherent instructions while, at the same time, dabbing away at the tears that were trickling down his cheeks. Only once we were out of the revolving doors of the chemist did Michael allow himself to explode with laughter. I have no doubt the pharmacist did the same.

In Hong Kong, we weren't short of entertainment in the evenings. The Lan Kwai Fong area provided us with bars and nightclubs, the most memorable being Joe Bananas. Ned Kelly's jazz club on Kowloon kept us happy for about half an hour, after which the cacophony of Dixieland jazz was enough to send us spiralling out onto the streets, eardrums pierced beyond repair. Until the next time.

We made sure to save a portion of our meal allowance for the horse races at Happy Valley. Sitting on cold concrete steps brought relief from the balmy evening. We placed our bets, got drunk on cheap lager, and even managed to win some money, before finally going home from Happy Valley, well … happy.

Even though I had done and seen as much as my feet and eyes could take, three nights was nowhere near enough time in Hong Kong. On the fourth morning, I reluctantly packed my bags for the second time since leaving Johannesburg, as we headed back to the airport for the flight to Taipei. This time, we had the luxury of flying as passengers on Cathay Pacific Airlines.

Taipei was nowhere near as glamorous as Hong Kong and the various markets a whole lot less salubrious. We started off the evening with a meal in the Genghis Kahn, a Mongolian barbeque not far from our hotel. I vaguely recognised the food we chose from a display of meats, vegetables and sauces. Not that I was an authority on distinguishing a sliver of house pet from the rump of a raging bull.

From there, we moved on to a karaoke bar. The room was dimly lit and painted in red. Animal hides and antlers adorned the walls. We sat on low sofas and cushions, around a square coffee table. Along one side of the room was a brightly lit bar and, on the opposite side, was a little stage with a raised platform under a small canopy. Microphones were set up for one or more singers. There was safety in numbers, especially if you couldn't sing. The bar was filled with patrons either drinking, singing, dancing, or simply milling around. I wondered if some of them might have been talent scouts in disguise.

Karaoke was a divertissement thus far unknown to me and which provided a great form of recreation. The Taiwanese people took it seriously. Unfortunately, we didn't. Our irreverent attitude to public singing in false keys, was met with indignation from the locals. I learnt many new versions to well-known songs. The words took on an inartistic, unrefined, slightly crude slant, which went a long way to ease the embarrassment of the moment. With a voice like mine, I'd rather be caught swearing than singing any day.

There are some things you only do once in life. A visit to the infamous Snake Alley is one of them. The taxi dropped us in front of a neon archway, with a long arcade. Nothing out of the ordinary. Until we stepped through the curved structure.

Snake Alley was plumb centre in the red-light district. Pornography shops and strippers lined the street on both sides. Many of the prostitutes were young, minors who had been sold into this sordid life by their parents. With glazed eyes, they solicited business wherever they saw an opportunity. It was pathetic and unspeakably sad. They tugged at the sleeves of our pilots, who popped a few dollar notes into their hungry hands and walked on, with no desire to indulge in their youthful flesh.

The name of the road is a dead give-away for the atrocities that took place there. Snakes in cages, snakes squirming as they hung from hooks, and others that wound themselves around the arms of their sellers, it was a continuous auction. Men with lapel mics fixed to their shirts, held these creatures aloft as they extolled the virtues of their blood, gall and every other body part. I had never witnessed such cruelty before. Nimble hands skinned the reptiles as they dangled and wriggled from hooks and ropes. Holding the writhing snakes aloft, they drained the blood and collected the gall in a cup. The highest bidder swallowed the vile liquid in one gulp. Apparently for medicinal reasons. Nausea clutched at my stomach.

It got worse. Monkeys tethered to custom-made wooden structures were scalped and hot oil poured into the gaping skulls. The highest bidders attacked this delicacy with teaspoons. By now, tears were streaming down my face.

I begged to be taken home, back to our hotel. But I wasn't swift enough to miss what appeared to be a cooking demonstration close to the exit of the alley. Giving a detailed explanation of the process, a young man drove a spike into the neck of a large terrapin, sliced its head off and added several ingredients to the body cavity before pouring the mixture into two shot glasses. Another aphrodisiac treat.

An orangutan in a little green sweater and matching shorts sat on a high bar stool. He clapped his hands sporadically and grinned as he oversaw the cruelty.

I didn't sleep that night. I twisted and turned, imagining every touch of the sheet a spitting cobra. Vivid images of the farcical tragedy of the evening haunted me. I knew then that I would never go back to that hideous street of macabre rituals and, for once, I looked forward to the prospect of going home.

6

FLYING FOR FREE

The perks of working in the travel industry, and in particular for an airline, were probably the reason most people either chose that line of work in the first place, or remained in it well after their sell-by date. Another reason was pressure from family members who faced the prospect of losing their own travel perks, if you get my drift. So, day after day, flight after flight, we donned our uniforms, dressed for battle in crisp shirts, dry-cleaned suits and heels high enough to induce vertigo in a tightrope walker. We did this all simply to satisfy those people dependent on us for their holidays – spouses, parents and siblings. These benefits did not extend to common-law husbands and wives, or partners. For obvious reasons, there was an ongoing campaign by the gay community in the airline, who in those days, would never have had a legal spouse. They did, however, seem to procure a variety of genetically modified long-lost brothers, with fictitious birth certificates, from obscurity. As the old expression goes, where there's a willy, there's a way. Not only were we there to provide our loved ones with a medley of either completely free, gratis air tickets or, at worst, an ID90, which meant they only paid ten per cent of the fare, but on board we generally ensured that they got upgraded if not to first class, then at least to business class. Plus … we usually managed to cajole the hotel management at the destination into stepping up the standard of our rooms to a suite or similar, in order to accommodate dependent family members. Only the best for our kith and kin.

The reason everybody was so keen to make use of the travel benefits was because some ignorant man once said that money spent on travel made you much happier than money spent on material goods. Well, I can only assume it had to have been a man. A woman would have said money spent on material goods whilst travelling made you happiest of all. I remember reading one time that there were supposedly ten major benefits to travel. There was some truth in it:

Travel improves social and communication skills: Crew needed no help with the social aspect and communication skills developed from, 'Would you like chicken or beef, Sir?' to 'Chiggenorbeef?'

Travel ensures peace of mind: This one was completely true. It was just that the wording needed adjusting slightly: Travel ensured that passengers got a piece of my mind.

Travel helps with original and creative thoughts: Crew were always very original in identifying a demanding passenger and extremely creative in telling them what to do with themselves.

Travel broadens your horizons: Unfortunately, it also broadened our waistlines.

Travel enhances your tolerance for uncertainty: That all depended on who was in control of the aircraft.

Travel boosts your confidence: Now when did a pilot ever lack confidence?

Travel gives you real-life education: Not the kind my father had in mind.

Travel creates memories for a lifetime: Some good, some bad, some vague.

Travel helps you have fun: Who needed travel when there was alcohol?

Travel helps you to get to know yourself: That was a last resort, only when nobody else wanted to get to know you.

I loved to take my mom on flights with me. She loved to travel. A lot. In fact, she was probably the reason that I never put my degree to good use in the first place – such was the influence of her wanderlust on my malleable child brain during the influential years of my childhood development. Freud would've had a ball.

She especially liked to go to Hong Kong with me. It was the chaos of the place. She may have been my mother, but we were total opposites when it came to the trivial traits like organisational skills, tidiness, punctuality and a quest for perfectionism. We were, however, identical when it came to the critical characteristics, such as zest for life, friendships and fondness for travel. There was one word – a simple 2-letter word – 'no' – that did not exist in her vocabulary when issued with an invitation. As long as it didn't involve dogs, or lifts; either at the same time, or individually. Now this may sound kinky, but such was the extent of her claustrophobia that she would opt to climb every single step to the top of the Empire State Building on crutches, rather than ensconce herself in a metal elevator. She was vocal about her fear of being enclosed in narrow spaces; definitely not a closet claustrophobic. As for the dogs … I never got to the bottom of that.

Talking about bottoms, on the flight from Mauritius to Hong Kong, she had her not inconsiderately sized bottom snugly compressed into a luxurious seat in business class. I had requested to work in that section of the cabin. Behind (can't get away from the rear ends when it came to my mother) her and next to her sat four businessmen.

The chaps were lovely and, whilst very chatty, they were not in the least bit demanding. All four of them were in the retail business and headed for various destinations in the Far East. There was safety in numbers, so I happily flirted along with all of them. That's what was nice about serving passengers in business class – you had the time to talk to and get to know people. A far cry from the race against time in cattle class. Turned out, they were staying in the same hotel as us. When they asked if I'd like to meet up with them for drinks in the hotel bar that evening, I declined, pointing out that the lady seated next to them was my mother, who was on the trip with me. 'Well,' they said, 'bring her along!' So, I did. To be fair, by the time we reached Hong Kong, she had forged a closer acquaintance with them than I had, anyway.

We checked into our hotel, into the upgraded luxury suite, naturally. After a short sleep and an obligatory awakening from deep slumber by a fire alarm midway through, we roused ourselves, hit the markets (that would be shopping, not Hang Seng) and made it back in time to the hotel bar for happy hour. Over frozen Margaritas and hot, buttery popcorn, an invitation was issued. The four men invited us to fly to Bangkok with them the next day. Naturally, we refused. But they were persistent, explaining that they would be out doing business (hmmm …) all day and would meet up with us in the evening to show us the sights. We had four days in Hong Kong, so one night squeezed in to visit Bangkok would work out rather nicely. But obviously not. There was definitely something sinister at play. Why on earth would four businessmen — make that four married businessmen — in fact, four happily married businessmen, they assured us — offer to fly a middle-aged lady and her daughter to an exotic destination, simply because they really enjoyed our company? The more they insisted over drinks and dinner, the more we resisted. We did, however, have a delightful evening filled with laughter. They appeared to be exceptionally nice people and it was hard to picture them as the sinister human traffickers, or drug dealers which they clearly were. Right up until the time we took ourselves off to bed, they were insistent on getting us to accept the offer of air tickets and hotel accommodation in Thailand. We never wavered in our refusal.

Getting ready to turn in, my mom and I discussed the strange offer from these extremely ordinary South African chaps and pondered their motivation. It seemed so innocent, yet it was too bizarre to be. We went to bed concluding that it had been a delightful evening nonetheless, as we made plans for getting the Star ferry and then the bus out to Stanley market on the Hong Kong side the following day. We wouldn't rush though, but would sleep in, without requesting a wake-up call. Fire alarms permitting.

In the morning I awoke, feeling slightly groggy as a result of both jet lag and margaritas. As I made my way to the bathroom, I spied a long white envelope peeking from underneath the door. I didn't really think too much of it, as the hotel sometimes popped these under our doors to warn us of a real fire drill, in which case we would be expected to evacuate our rooms in any state of undress, as opposed to simply sitting out the alarm or some similar event. Sometimes, it was even an invitation from the hotel management requesting our presence at a cocktail party. However, on this occasion, inside this envelope lurked two Cathay Pacific air tickets, as well as a voucher for the Mandarin Oriental hotel. I was horrified. I shook my mom awake and we stared in disbelief at the contents. Now what? We could either view this gift as a covert invitation to join the dark underworld of drugs and murder, or perhaps God was trying to thank us in His own way for being such a wonderful pair who brought joy to people wherever we went. After much discussion, we opted for the latter. So, an hour later, we found ourselves in a taxi en route to the airport for the flight to Bangkok per kind favour of four men whose surnames we did not even know.

A driver was at Bangkok airport to meet us, with my name displayed on a white board. He drove us to the spectacular hotel, situated right on the river. We kept giggling nervously, unable to shrug off the feelings of scepticism and suspicion. We still weren't quite sure how we had found ourselves in this position and wondered how we would ever explain this to anybody, not least my father, who also happened to be the husband of my mother. If we didn't end up in some filthy Thai prison for acting as drug mules, that is. Blame it on a healthy dose of naivety.

When we checked in, there was a note for me, saying that they (always plural) would meet us in the foyer at six that evening. We debated whether just to enjoy the day in Bangkok and do a runner before it was time to meet them in the evening.

We dropped our overnight bags in the luxury room and headed off on a boat excursion recommended by the concierge. A long-tailed speedboat took us down the river, along the multitude of winding canals. It was this that earned Bangkok the title of Venice of the East. The return journey, on a rice boat, offered a glimpse of authentic riverside lifestyles, as we glided past houses on stilts and children playing in the water, and indulged in soft drinks and unusual seasonal fruits.

The four men were probably more surprised at seeing us in the foyer that evening than we had been at their invitation. But they seemed genuinely delighted. They hailed a tuk-tuk and we set off to experience the nightlife in Bangkok. After dinner, we headed to the notorious Go-Go bars that I had always heard of. The place where it had all started and one of the world's most famous red light districts, was Patpong. Alongside a night market teeming with hawkers and humble stalls, was the neon-lit strip of bars offering naughty shows and a variety of adult entertainment. An aging prostitute sidled up to us, hooked an arm through that of one of 'our' men and breathed, 'Hello Sar, love is calling.' It might have been, but it definitely wasn't calling his name. I learnt all about Ladyboys and discovered many ways of dispelling ping pong balls, smoking cigarettes and how to pop a balloon with a flying dart. Just the kind of skills required to get you through life.

One of the funniest things that I recall from that night was being handed a brochure by a grubby-looking hotelier doing a hard sell. I still have this leaflet, which I guard as fiercely as my jewellery box, for its invaluable ability to bring me out of the depths of any hint of depression. This is how it reads:

Getting there:
Our representative will make you wait at the airport. The bus to the hotel runs along the lake shore. Soon you will feel pleasure in passing water. You will know that you are getting near the hotel, because you will go round the bend. The manager will await you in the entrance hall. He always tries to have intercourse with all new guests.

The Hotel:
This is a family hotel, so children are very welcome. We of course are always pleased to accept adultery. Highly skilled nurses are available to put down your children. Guests are invited to conjugate in the bar and expose themselves to others. But please note that ladies are not allowed to have babies in the bar. We organize social games, so no guest is ever left alone to play with them self.

The Restaurant:
Our menus have been carefully chosen to be ordinary and unexciting. At dinner, our quartet will circulate from table to table, and fiddle with you.

Your Room:
Every room has excellent facilities for your private parts. In winter, every room is on heat. Each room has a balcony

offering views of outstanding obscenity! You will not be disturbed by traffic noise, since the road between the hotel and the lake is used only by pederasts.

Bed:
Your bed has been made in accordance with local tradition. If you have any other ideas please ring for the chambermaid. Please take advantage of her. She will be very pleased to squash your shirts, blouses and underwear. If asked, she will also squeeze your trousers.

Above All:
When you leave us at the end of your holiday you will have no hope. You will struggle to forget it.

Patently, this was either a direct translation from Thai, or perhaps they were advertising a hotel with fringe benefits.

The evening was delightful and above all, educational. We still could not fathom the generosity displayed by these men, who clearly expected nothing in return. They insisted that they thoroughly enjoyed our company, as well as the warm relationship that existed between mother and daughter, and would not have had nearly as many laughs without us. The four of them regularly travelled together for long stints, which apparently grew tiresome. Any light-hearted diversion was welcome, even at their own cost. Why did they not take their own wives along then? That, apparently, would be more tiresome. Who were we to question this?

At the end of the evening we said our goodbyes, thanked them profusely for their generosity and did not swop telephone numbers. They would be off doing their business early in the morning and we would fly back to Hong Kong in the late afternoon. Prior to departing for the airport, we considered ditching our hand luggage and handbags and flying simply with the clothes on our backs and our passports, such was our mistrust. I was convinced that, somehow, they might have managed to plant drugs or something equally sinister upon our beings. And yet, they were such regular blokes, who seemed sincere … and extremely wealthy. I turned our bags inside out, undid zips, looked suspiciously into lipstick tubes and finally declared us safe. We decided to accept it all at face value.

Only once we'd made it successfully through the airport building and onto the plane, could we relax and marvel at this weird experience that most people would probably view in a very cynical light. To this day, I cannot explain why they did it, or why we accepted the offer. Either way, we landed safely in Hong Kong and the rest, as they say, is mystery.

7

DEN OF INIQUITY

The infamous island of Ilha do Sal in the Cape Verde was bad. But in a good way, depending on how high your morals were. I'd heard that this place had an uncapped ability to play host to the most debauched parties. It might have just been a rumour but still, I couldn't wait to see it. Purely to satisfy my curiosity, obviously.

Where most crew were battling to avoid this tedious destination, I was desperate to get there. I knew it wouldn't take long, because not many people volunteered for flights that included a layover in Sal, so I'd whispered in the roster clerk's ear. There was a risk though, because now that he'd found a willing volunteer, there was every chance that I would find myself headed for that isle of ill repute for the rest of my natural life.

In the history of the airline, only one or maybe two staff members had ever been fired for not adhering to the 'eight hours between bottle and throttle' rule. Both these dismissals were consequences of late-night partying on Sal Island. Rules are rules, but, given the choice, I would rather have flown with a pilot who had one or two drinks under his belt than a hungover one. The intoxicated one would have been doing his utmost to appear 100 per cent sober. I knew he would be concentrating really hard on the matter at hand. He would be focussed. I'd seen guys arriving for a flight with a monumental hangover that not even an eight-hour sleep could begin to obliterate. They were within the rules, but with a hangover hitting 8.9 on the Richter scale they couldn't really care less whether they lived or died. Which translated into they couldn't really care if I lived or died, either. Give me the inebriated aviator any day.

One pilot, who was known to over-indulge rather frequently, was asked the question, 'Why do you drink so much?' His response, 'Because I'm scared of flying,' was met with sympathy. 'But then, why on earth did you become a pilot?' His reply 'Because I like drinking,' was not.

They say that everything comes to those who wait. Long enough. It did. When I returned from one of my international flights, I checked my roster and found – much to my delight – that my next fight would include an Ilha do Sal layover en route to New York. Finally I was going to experience this nefarious island, which was a bit like the proverbial Marmite, adored or despised, with absolutely no middle road. It was hallowed by those who liked to party, as well as by those on the opposite end of the spectrum who enjoyed nature and the serenity to be found in the remoteness and lack of sophistication. But the serious shoppers and club-and theatre-goers could be heard shedding bitter tears of frustration down the passages of the Cabin Services building, if they returned from a flight to find the airport code 'SID' anywhere on their roster. To these city-slickers, it would be two or three days of purgatory before setting foot in the hustle and bustle of the Big Apple. It was hard for them to accept that they couldn't have one without the other. Poor spoiled brats. My heart bled for them. How unreasonable to expect them to spend a day or two on the sun-bleached shores of the Atlantic Ocean.

The reason these miserable people were subjected to the odd night on Ilha do Sal was because in the apartheid days, when South Africa was still persona non grata in the political arena, the airline was forced to fly around the bulge of Africa. For non-geographers, that's the left side of the continent, about two thirds up. Many of the African countries were not keen to give away air space to a white-supremacy-owned airline. This resulted in many of the long-haul international flights having to make a refuelling stop en route to Europe and the USA, which extended the travelling time, for example, to London, by around three hours. It also meant that, due to the long flights and a host of flight and duty regulations, our layovers at various destinations were anywhere between three days and seventeen, due to the weekly frequency. South African Airways maintained extensive international links despite sanctions, and despite this overfly ban. However, there were certain periods when SAA was banned altogether from landing in the United States and Australia, due to the comprehensive Anti-Apartheid Act. Most of the bans were lifted at the end of apartheid in 1990 and services to former destinations resumed and new destinations in Africa and Asia were introduced. This drastically reduced our layovers on outbound trips, as the frequency of flights increased. South African aircraft were even finally allowed to enter Egyptian and Sudanese airspace.

Understandably, there was fierce international opposition to apartheid, especially in the 1980s, which resulted in, amongst other things, SAA's offices being targeted. In London, the airline's offices were daubed in red paint and protesters went on the rampage in other parts of the world at various times. It's true that during the apartheid era, very few non-white South Africans could afford to fly. There was never any segregation or discrimination on board, or at the airport, as this was classified an 'international' facility and thus was not subject to the provisions of the Separate Amenities Act. The same was true for major hotels and shopping malls. Until the late '80s, the crew were all white, due to the fact that SAA was owned by the South African Railways, which imposed a policy of job reservation. This started to change in 1985, when SAA began recruiting local Asian and Indian females. By 1989, all race and gender groups were hired. This included Taipei-based Chinese girls, who acted as public relations officers on board due to the vast loads of non-English speaking passengers on those routes.

In general, as crew, we were all liberal in our political outlook; this was enhanced by travel, which gave us an insight into other cultures and worlds, but was also possibly due to our youth and open-mindedness.

The moment had arrived: I was finally about to set foot on Sal island. From my jump seat next to the window, I had a clear view of the brightly lit-up runway on our approach. As we came closer and closer to touch-down, I pressed my nose to the porthole. Instead of the typically sterile tarmac that stretched out like a strip of plaster, normally secured from human and mechanical intervention on landing, a collection of feral dogs and cats scattered in all directions from beneath the belly of this beast. The older hostie next to me didn't bat an eyelid, so I tried to appear equally unfazed. I could tell she was one of those sorry ones who didn't want to be landing here. The way she said 'fuck it' was a dead give-away.

We landed safely, not a flattened dog in sight. As the plane taxied to the bay, we remained on our jump seats, waiting for the overhead lights to be switched off. If only passengers were as obedient. The minute the plane hit the deck, half of them climbed out of their seats. 'Ladies and Gentlemen, for your own safety, please remain seated until the aircraft has come to a complete stop.' Five seconds later, 'Ladies and Gentlemen, I *said* for your own safety…' Thirty seconds later, 'For Christ's sake, Ladies and Gentlemen …' Well, that's what I would have said, if I had been the senior bag on this flight reading the announcements.

The new, fresh crew boarded – most of them looking not so fresh. Dark bags hung from below their eyes and alcohol dripped from their pores. Amidst lots of air kissing and loud shrieks, they recounted intimate details of their stay. Some of the passengers found these scandalous conversations, describing various tales of reprehensible behaviour, completely captivating. They arched their necks and rubbed their hands together in morbid fascination, straining for even more titbits of profligacy. However, it's important to point out that while some revered us, this behaviour didn't sit well with the majority of the passengers who were already irritated at having been woken up for the landing at around two in the morning. Nobody likes to be told to sit upright and fasten their seatbelt anywhere after midnight. One gentleman, in particular, displayed rather ambiguous behaviour, which involved him placing his head very close to mine and baring his teeth in what I assumed was a grin. I was wrong; he was furious. That, I find, is another problem with passengers. The inconsistency. You can never tell if a person is going to offer you his left kidney, or smash you in the face with his forehead.

We continued with the handover rituals, advising the new crew of the assortment of 'preps' that had been done, special meals to be handed out and surreptitiously giving them a detailed – generally disparaging – rundown on various passengers. We finally disembarked the few people who were not continuing on to New York, collected our luggage from the foot of the aircraft steps, cleared customs, and headed for the crew bus. This all took less than five minutes, as the airport terminal consisted of a rickety little cement block with one official, who stamped our passports. He had the extraordinary ability to match our faces to our photographs without ever looking up.

I was surprised to discover that the cockpit crew were already at the bus and a few of them had changed into their running kit as they loaded their bags. They told me that this was customary amongst some of the keen runners, as the hotel was only 17km from the airport. Well, that was absolutely super for these astronauts, who had spent the previous eight hours with their bottoms stuck to a seat, or their entire bodies prostrate on a bunk in the crew rest. Cabin crew had, by that stage, already pretty much completed an entire marathon. Another 17km would have been a stretch too far for my weary legs. With not a trace of envy, I sank into my seat at the back of the bus.

The moon was full and ripe, and I fell instantly in love with this place. It was beautiful. Stark and unsophisticated, Sal Island had an eerie allure in the white moonshine. It's an arid island and almost flat. I came to understand why this made it popular amongst those of us who called ourselves runners – both the flatness of it, as well as the ability to host wild parties. The magical journey in the glow of the moon ended all too soon. I couldn't wait to discover this unspoilt beauty by the light of early dawn.

We arrived at the charming but very basic Hotel Morabeza. I have to concede that perhaps it was the moonlight that added to the enchantment. By day, it turned out to be a warren of mismatched stone buildings, originally constructed as a second home by a Belgian industrialist, due to the wonderful climate. In the early 1960s, the airline undertook an experimental flight and subsequently landed on Ilha do Sal. After repairs were made to the landing strip, a regular flight between Johannesburg and Frankfurt started, with the requisite stopover in Sal. Initially, the arrangement had been to rent two rooms at this large private home for the crew layover but, in time, more accommodation was needed and one thing led to another, with more and more prefabricated rooms being constructed. Later, additional rooms were built using the local rocks until, due to the rising demand from the airline, which made Ilha do Sal its major stopover worldwide with up to thirty-two Boeing 747s per week, the Morabeza became a 140-room hotel!

We lined up in the dimly lit reception area to receive our room keys. The lobby was sparse, with none of the customary soft, puffy sofas to relax on, not to mention a dearth of waiters hovering around with a long-stemmed glass of sparkling wine and certainly no freshly scented moist towels to wipe our overworked hands with. We stood around, chatting as we waited. I was surprised to find there was no meal allowance payout. The older crew explained that we wouldn't be able to spend it, as there were neither restaurants nor shops in the village. I wondered how the community survived. The local currency had no value and it was, in fact, illegal to take it off the island on departure. I could never understand the reasoning behind that and never met a soul who did. For this reason, our subsistence and travel allowance would be paid back at base in South African currency. We ate breakfast, lunch and supper in the hotel's modest dining room. I mentally prepared myself for a diet of fish. I hadn't seen an edible animal so far, and I couldn't imagine what vegetables or fruit could be grown in this infertile desert terrain. I was cautiously optimistic about finding chicken on the menu, though. They were tough birds, which seemed to thrive in these sort of adverse conditions. Fortunately, the bar accepted foreign currency, which proved no problem for airline crew.

I'm not sure if the hotel management thought that we were in the business of trading with hotel room keys, but they certainly ensured that this would be an impossible venture. Each key had what looked like an entire tree attached to it in the form of a massive wooden knob. I couldn't begin to fathom where all this wood came from on this barren island, with not a twig to be seen in the middle of a single salt pan. I couldn't decide which was heavier – my key ring or my suitcase.

It was about three in the morning local time. After spending approximately eight hours on my feet serving passengers, I was totally exhausted and dying to put my head on a pillow. However, before this could be achieved, I had a few more obstacles to overcome. The first challenge was getting my suitcase to my room. The walkways to the accommodation block consisted of shale and cobbles. It was an awkward journey, as the suitcase wheels could not find purchase on the pebbles. Teetering in high heels, I had to lug 23kg of wobbling clothing, hairdryer, cosmetics, and a few more unmentionables, behind me. At this ungodly hour, it felt like hiking the Camino trail. At least my keyring in the other hand balanced me, as it matched the weight of my suitcase.

My bedroom was distinctly lacking in luxury, housing just a narrow, single bed. No chocolate on the pillow. No plump duvet. Certainly no waffle-weave robe and matching slippers hanging behind the door. An unattractive brown wardrobe, which threatened to topple over on opening, revealed a solitary, buckled, wire, coat hanger – the kind you get back from the drycleaners and immediately dump in the bin. Instead of 100 per cent Egyptian cotton bed linen, all that I could find on my bed was an animal-like furry throw. This had pride of place at the end of the bed, on top of a not-so-crisp sheet. The thought did cross my mind that perhaps the locals had found a use for all the feral cats after all. The windows had a layer of gauze where one would have expected glass. At least it had a wooden door. With a lock. Hence the keys.

I could cope with this modest bedroom, being as tired as I was, as long as it was clean. I went to inspect the bathroom, which apparently had only recently been converted from salt- to freshwater showers. I could think of nothing worse than having to get into bed saline-sticky, with hair stiff as a wooden plank. Ever the optimist, I peeked around the door hoping against my better judgement to find an array of shampoos, luxury bubble bath, shower cap, sewing kit and an assortment of emery boards and cotton wool balls. Hell, I'm no stranger to disappointment.

I had a quick shower and, despite the tempting peals of laughter to which my gauze window offered no resistance, I decided to forgo the debriefing party which, by the sound of it, was in full swing, and opted instead for a couple of hours of blissful oblivion. For once, the idea of waking up restored and invigorated overrode my fear of missing out. I couldn't wait to fall into a deeply induced coma.

Approaching the unpretentious little bed, I spotted a cockroach the size of a small elephant on my pillow staring at me. I was determined not to be the one to look away first. He didn't blink once. A type of guerrilla warfare ensued. Eventually, I was forced to pick up the pillow at one end and thrash it against the wall in order to confound the malicious little being. It clung to the pillow with the ferocity of a crab, as it challenged me to the right of a good night's sleep. 'I'm going to smash your head in,' I said. 'Oh no, you're not,' it replied. For the record, I was the victor on that occasion. Why didn't Noah just crush those two loathsome cockroaches when he had the opportunity?

Ilha do Sal was even more beautiful by day. The white sand beach stretched on endlessly, enticing me to go for a long walk. The sea was a whirling motion of aquamarine, cobalt and azure blue. It was tempting to enter the water, but there were no shark nets and, as I walked along the rickety little pier, sharks swam around in abundance, while the local fishermen gutted their catch of the day.

This was a destination of 'anything goes'. Because it was totally barren, isolated, sparsely populated and always hot, there was absolutely nothing to do to keep the crew amused. We had more chance of discovering a pedigree dog on the island than a jet ski. The closest we came to water sports later that day was a foray out into the blue yonder, on a leaking little fishing vessel hired for the princely sum of two beers.

The island as I knew it then, with its rustic charm, is a memory to be cherished forever. The intervention of tourism has changed it beyond recognition. Hotels now litter the lunar landscape. Restaurants clamour for Michelin status, while al fresco cafés line the once deserted beaches. Music blares out over sun loungers and brollies. The ocean is dotted with catamarans, windsurfers, water-skiers and whale-watching boats. Activities range from snooker to paintballing. The serenity of this erstwhile paradise has been infinitely destroyed.

Aeroflot, Russian Airlines, was the only other airline whose aircrew patronised the hotel on a permanent basis during the Cold War period. It was clear that the Aeroflot crew had been given the instruction that there was to be absolutely no interaction with their western counterparts. This was a challenge we South Africans could not turn our backs on, doing all that was in our power to elicit just a flicker of a smile.

In the heat of the afternoon, a group of us sat on the hotel's rustic veranda, not far from the Aeroflot pilots, enjoying a few drinks. Determined to get some kind of response, we smiled, we waved, we even got one of our party to strip down to the bare minimum and do a seductive belly dance within touching distance of them, but there was still not a hint of interest. The fact that this go-go girl was a fleshy, overweight man in a Speedo probably didn't help our cause, but it was worth a try. We weren't expecting them to make a pass, but a laugh would've been good.

Nothing worked. Unwilling to give up, the South African blokes huddled together and came up with a plan. They decided to set their opposition a challenge of strength that they knew the Russians would not be able to resist. Screw-top beer bottles were the latest innovation in South Africa. The male members of our crew had brought beers along for the layover and started making a show of opening them on the flesh of their inner arms, while grinning at the opposition and then toasting them. They made it look effortless, but it couldn't have been easy. The Russians decided to break protocol. It was not an option for them to take this show of strength lying down. Determined to match our boys, they ordered the local (unwittingly – non-screw top) beers from the hotel and attempted to replicate the actions of the South Africans by using the soft flesh of their inner arms to open the beers. They groaned and grunted determinedly, but unsuccessfully. Finally, with incomprehension written all over their broad foreheads, arms shredded and dripping with blood and not a single open beer, they filed into line behind their commissar and disappeared into the dusk.

There are further legends that tell of late-night drinking parties between the two sets of pilots, which culminated in the South Africans appearing for their flight to Johannesburg kitted out in Aeroflot uniforms – though the Russian crew were never spotted sporting the grey-blue uniforms of our pilots. One can only wonder what their fate might have been. Salt mines in Siberia springs to mind.

The lack of any laid-on entertainment meant that we had to find ways of amusing ourselves. This wasn't difficult. It always started the same way. With alcohol. Lots of it. We all knew that booze didn't solve the world's problems but then again, neither did milk. It always ended the same way too: passing out from alcohol. And then, what felt like a few minutes later, which always happened to be around one in the morning, it was time to get ready to head back to the airport for the next sector of the flight.

This gave rise to a regular, but no less amusing set of circumstances. Since the Morabeza Hotel lacked the sophistication of even the most basic telephone system, there was no option of an automated wake-up call for crew members to ensure that everyone turned up on time for the scheduled departure to the airport. Instead, this was facilitated on a manual basis. The local security guard was a delightful Creole man named Shorty. Well, that's what the crew called him, based on his stature. For as long as I knew him, he was never seen without the elaborate gold-braided cap given to him by one of our pilots in the early days. Probably because it added 6in to his height. Shorty neither spoke nor understood a word of English but moonlighted as an alarm clock, night after night after night. Lying in my bed on my first night-stop in Sal, I was gently woken by the repetitive series of calls coming ever closer down the cobbled walkway to my very own gauze window. This is how it went: Knock. Knock. Knock. 'Calling time.' 'Fuck off, Shorty!' 'Thank you, Sir.' Knock. Knock. Knock. 'Calling time.' 'Fuck off, Shorty!' 'Thank you, Sir.' Knock. Knock. Knock. 'Calling time.' 'Fuck off, Shorty!' 'Thank you, Sir.' Eventually, everybody boarded the bus on time.

8

SUICIDE ON THE SLOPES

I had been privileged as a 10-year-old child to experience the thrill of skiing. Not water-skiing, which most South African children learn to do before they learn to walk, but the act of donning clunky boots attached to long, slender runners made of wood intended for gliding over snow. Being geographically so far removed from Europe, or any destination that offered snow skiing, meant that very few South African children were lucky enough to be taken on this type of holiday.

I remember arriving in the picturesque village of Villars, nestled high in the Swiss Alps. My brother, who was a year older than me, and I felt as if we had been dropped into the fairy-tale world of Hansel and Gretel. Only, there were no witches here, just elegant people speaking a language we couldn't understand. Our hosts were gracious. They were the elderly parents of a couple who were both doctors at the missionary hospital near our home. Jean and Simone and their two daughters had become very close family friends of ours, in our rural hometown of Bushbuck Ridge.

Theirs was the quintessential wooden alpine chalet, where we indulged in bircher muesli and cheese fondues. We learnt to ski by day and spent some of the afternoons ice skating on an open-air ice rink, surrounded by icing-sugar-covered mountains with the strains of Lara's Theme from *Doctor Zhivago* ringing in our ears. It was a song I recognised, because our parents used to play it often in our car. Not via Bluetooth, mind you, but rather via one of those enormous cassettes that resembled the Encyclopaedia Britannica, which got shoved into a gaping recess somewhere under the dashboard.

My next skiing experience would be many years later during a university break. That holiday ignited my passion for the sport, so I was delighted to find that the airline was going to be magnanimous enough to sponsor my future exposure to this recreational activity on a very regular basis and to a variety of venues.

The skiing community in the airline clamoured to be rostered on ten-day Zurich flights, as soon as the season got started. A ten-day flight, in effect, gave us eight days at the destination, with a day in the middle when we would do a shuttle to another European city, such as Brussels or Amsterdam. Very inconvenient. Sometimes, we'd have two days before the shuttle and five days after. Either way, there was always enough time to hit the slopes.

Lizzy and I had put in our request well in advance. It would've been unusual not to have other skiers on the flight but, to be on the safe side, I always requested one of these flights with a friend, or sometimes a whole group of us requested the same flights to be sure we would have playmates in the Alps, the Sierra Nevada, the Black Forest and even the Snowy Mountains in Oz.

With my snowsuit, moonboots, gloves, socks and goggles hogging 95 per cent of my suitcase, I headed to the airport for the flight to Zurich. If I hadn't been so excited at the prospect of skiing, I don't think I would have survived that outbound journey. Some flights are just like that. I'm sure there's a place where they advertise half-price air tickets with the prerequisite that you have to be a demanding, miserable git. Otherwise, how would you find 272 like-minded, difficult passengers with not a drop of humour between them? But then again, they were Swiss. If you had taken a civil servant from every state department, from any country in the world, and squashed them all into this one Jumbo Jet, you probably would have had more chance of wresting a flicker of happiness. Well, maybe that's an exaggeration.

The flight was full. Passengers lined the aisles, as they struggled to find their seats. It didn't take a massive IQ to understand the way the row numbers increased from the front to the back of the plane, yet many people seemed overwhelmed by this chronological arrangement. They stared at their boarding passes, then craned their necks to get a glimpse of the row numbers. If there was anyone sitting in what they presumed to be their seat, they repeated this exercise until help arrived in the form of an air hostess.

A self-important young couple stood in the aisle, boarding passes in hand, blocking the way forward for the other four million grumpy passengers. Their only obvious talent was chewing gum, teeth gnashing through their open mouths. They didn't give a hoot; they were intent on finding their seats and were prepared to take as long as it took. That was the problem with economy-class passengers. They thought they'd bought the entire plane. Bubblegum Lady planted her platform heels on either side of a most definitely non-regulation-size piece of hand luggage, arms folded. Bubblegum Man, hands coiled into fists, leaned right into the faces of the elderly folk who, he assumed, were occupying his seats. 'Show me your boarding passes,' he barked. The row behind was empty.

I did not like this obnoxious pair; they had no endearing qualities. Especially the man. His shirt buttons were undone almost to his navel and there was a heavy gold chain around his neck. I know that's not a reason to dislike someone, but why the hell not?

The old lady's hand fluttered to her mouth. Her husband rose from the seat, as they started the slow process of extricating themselves in preparation to move to the row behind. By now, the crowd lining the aisle were more than fidgeting and coughing; they were starting to hurl abuse.

I needed to get my hands on the semi bare-chested, gold-chained menace. I climbed over bodies and under legs and finally managed to get myself closer to the site of the altercation. If I had not intervened at this point there would have been bloodshed, so angry was the gum-chewing male. Things weren't moving quickly enough for him. The pressure of the crowd was getting to him. I asked the older people for their boarding passes, which the gentleman handed over with a trembling hand. 'I'm so sorry,' he said. I took the ticket stubs from the hand, with its creased skin and tired blue veins popping out like silkworms.

I glanced at the numbers printed on the piece of paper, 'You're perfectly correct. Stay where you are; you are in the right seats.' I felt an overwhelming urge to hug the frail, old man. At least now I had a valid reason to dislike the loathsome couple.

I then asked Mr Uber-confident to hand over his tickets. I grabbed him by his gold chain and turned him around. Well, that's what I felt like doing. It gave me great pleasure to send them off to the very last row of the plane, right in front of the galley bulkhead. I was going to make sure we clattered stowages and banged metal pots all night. I briefly considered relieving the wife of her oversized cabin bag, but I didn't; no need to push things. I'm nice that way.

A family of five boarded the plane. I could spot trouble when I saw it. At their head was a stocky gentleman with a head so square that it resembled a cardboard box. That alone was enough to cause my windpipe to shut down with fear. His bowed arms pumped the air as he strode towards me, with eyebrows that sat on his forehead like two angry caterpillars.

'Zisss isss ridiculoussss,' he hissed into my face. I almost turned and ran. I thought about locking myself into the toilet, fearing that he was a dead Romanian dictator come back to life. Instead, I politely asked him what the problem was. Turns out their seats were scattered from the wingtips to the tail of the plane. Two adults and three young children. Ground staff had assured him it would all be sorted out on board. They would say anything to get rid of an angry passenger before things got ugly. That's why we didn't like the ground staff. And they'd only had this Ceauşescu-esque character for five or ten minutes. I was facing twelve hours in his company.

I was so afraid of this man, I would have seated them all in the cockpit if I'd had to. With the help of a couple of my colleagues, we managed to switch people around, making promises we would never keep, and finally settled them in relatively close proximity to one another. But still not close enough for his liking. You'd think he would have been grateful.

Any flight that is filled with infants is going to be a bad one. From the minute we took to the air, the wailing started.

The cabin reverberated under a barrage of mournful crying. The decibel levels rose steadily. A few hours into the flight and everybody was getting irritated. This was not a privilege reserved for the crew only. Most of the mothers ignored the angry glares directed at them. Either they were totally oblivious to this cacophony streaming forth out of the gaping wounds that were their infants' mouths, or they had simply mastered the art of feigning death. For some reason known only to a higher being, passengers not encumbered with children of their own, turned to us and said, 'Do something with the baby.' Having this request directed at me by a humourless man, seated next to a woman who had assumed the aforesaid death-like pose and had all but abandoned her child, I picked up the howling tot. The mother never even challenged me. I could have kidnapped that bairn. Escape in this instance might have proved a problem. Besides which, given the choice of swimming the English Channel with a broken arm or spending the rest of my life with this kid, I would have started pulling on my bathing suit without a second's hesitation.

I walked up and down the dark aisle, tripping over stray legs and feet, but nothing could stop the bellowing which emanated from this minute person. Henry, the chief steward working in my section, leaned out of the galley and stopped me as I was completing my fourth circuit of the plane. 'Come here, Doll,' he said, hauling me behind the curtains, 'get her bottle.' I made my way back to where I had found the baby and asked the mother for her bottle. It was at this point that I thought that perhaps the woman might show some interest as to the welfare of her child. I couldn't have been more wrong. She handed me the plastic bottle with neither suspicion nor gratitude.

Henry unscrewed the top, emptied a miniature of Bailey's liqueur into the bottle and filled it with milk. He then placed the bottle into a stainless steel jug of boiling water to warm the concoction. The infant thrashed about in my arms, yelling. Henry had done this before. He removed the bottle from the heat, splashed a few drops on his wrist, declared it lukewarm and placed the teat in the tiny mouth. The result was instant. Not death, but sleep. (Don't worry – he didn't really do this, but he did put a drop of Rooibos tea and a healthy dose of sugar into the milk. A more efficient remedy has yet to be invented).

While we were doping babies, other crew members were dealing with a different crisis. A belligerent man was shouting and gesticulating from the rear of the plane. He had clearly consumed more alcohol than the daily recommended amount suggested by any Medical Association. He insisted on sitting on the door bustle to have a smoke, despite being politely informed of the danger this posed. The last thing we needed was an escape slide to inflate into the interior of the plane. The plane was full, so there was not an option of moving him to a smoking seat. Besides which, it was never a good idea to leave a drunken smoker unattended. Slack-jawed and slightly slumped over, he rested his large frame against the door. His trousers had slid down, revealing the start of the crack at the top of his bottom. 'Leavemealone. Justgetmeadrink.'

'You want a drink? Sure, Sir, what would you like? Another whiskey?' That's when Freddie decided he'd had enough. 'Let's Rhoda him, Doll,' he said. In airline parlance, to Rhoda somebody was a euphemism for popping a quarter of a sleeping tablet into the drink of an unsuspecting drunk and disorderly passenger. Well, it was either that or a stun gun. This was a last resort, purely for safety reasons, of course. Fortunately, by the time we got back to him, he'd already passed out so there was no need to administer the lethal concoction.

I never got to sit down for the entire period that I was on duty that night. Every single time I tried to make it from one end of the aisle to the other in response to a call bell, some shadowy form tugged at my pinny. The demands were more than I could cope with. I must have promised twenty-four Scotches, ten beers, five packets of nuts and a partridge in a pear tree. The only time I did actually approach a poorly-looking character out of concern and ask, 'Is everything alright? Can I get you some water?' his response, 'Yes please, with Scotch,' made me want to set fire to his sideburns.

What was left of the flight proceeded without further incident, other than an emergency landing without a nose wheel. (Not true, but it wouldn't have surprised me one bit – that's just how I was expecting that flight to end.)

We landed in Switzerland, grumpy and tired. I stepped off the plane and my heart dropped at the sight of the endless, shiny, tiled passage that would lead us through immigration and to our luggage. I doubted I had the energy, or the inclination, to complete that journey on foot. Praise the Lord, it looked as if there were escalators, if you stared hard enough at the horizon. Respite was in sight. With our wobbly legs, the crew stood in an ascending line as we travelled slowly and bumpily up the long, moving stairway. On our left, passengers who, on the contrary, were dying to stretch their legs after various long flights, bounced up the solid, tiled staircase, taking two steps at a time, showing off their vigour for our benefit, no doubt. I couldn't even muster a smirk. However, the scenario playing out on the other side of us was enough to make me forget about my fatigue, as I watched a James Bond *doppelgänger*, impatient with the crowds, ascend the downward-bound escalator. The well-heeled and suited man, briefcase in hand, had started his journey to beat the crowds on what he assumed was an out-of-order conveyer. He ran up the stationary steps like a gazelle. It worked like a charm for the first two-thirds of the excursion but, suddenly, the motor kicked in and the stairs started their downward journey. As 007 was now so close to the top, he was determined to reach the peak. He might as well have been climbing Kilimanjaro backwards. Like a hamster on a wheel, he ran and ran but got nowhere. Briefcase flapping madly by his side, the stuntman eventually succumbed to mechanics. Amidst much clapping and whooping (from the non-Helvetians only, naturally), he made his way to the bottom of the stairs in embarrassed silence, where he had no option but to use the more conventional way up. This time his demeanour more closely resembled Mister Bean than Mister Bond.

After this entertaining interlude, we finally made it to our hotel in Zurich. The city lies at the north end of the magnificent lake. The luxurious, five-star Hilton was in the centre of the business district, close to Paradeplatz. It's hard to understand how living in such a magnificently beautiful environment is still not enough to bring joy to a population. I got the impression the Swiss were reluctant to share this beauty with tourists by the way they tried to make every experience as unpleasant for us as possible. Even their response to ordering a cup of coffee felt like an attempt to get rid of us. Little did they know, we were not going to be deterred that easily. Far more effort would be required.

A couple of us met up in the foyer of the hotel after a few hours' sleep, to go for a meal and plan our skiing trip. There was another full crew staying over in the same hotel on the second part of their ten-day layover. A few of them had been coerced into joining us, both for dinner as well as for the outing to Flumserberg the following day. As it was new to me, I wanted to explore a bit of this exquisite city. Unfortunately, this culminated in me being taken via Needle Park en route to the old city. Not quite as bad as Snake Alley, but not in an altogether different league either. Nowadays cleaned up and known as Platzspitz Park, this was where heroin addicts frequently gathered in the 1980s. Any attempts at dispersing them simply resulted in them regrouping elsewhere. So, despite the disciplined nature of the Swiss, in 1987 they actually condoned the illegal use and sales of drugs in this park. The authorities declared that police weren't allowed to enter or make arrests and, believe it or not, clean needles were actually given to addicts. They *gave* them needles! Call me old-fashioned, but I viewed that as encouragement, or at least as sanctioning of the habit. This exercise was labelled the ZIPP-AIDS programme – the Zurich Intervention Pilot Project. What might have sounded like a good idea on paper unsurprisingly went pear-shaped in practice, due to lack of control of what went on in the park. Inevitably drug dealers and users arrived in their hordes from all over Europe. Dealers fought for control and addicts turned to theft to support their habit. Crime was rampant. The emergency services were overwhelmed with treating overdoses and other related incidents, until the park was finally cleared up by the police in 1992.

The others had seen it before and had no desire to get too close themselves as they pushed Lizzy and me deeper into the park. They hovered on the outskirts, close enough to keep an eye on us. I had no idea what I was letting myself in for, but had a feeling it wasn't going to be pleasant. The light in the late afternoon was growing dusky. As we stepped further into the park, the light grew dimmer, with patches of sunlight pushing their way through pine trees and other foliage. But there was enough light for me to see the young chap, leaning against a bench, right next to me. He had a belt knotted so tightly around the top of his arm that I could see the turgid vein. It bulged and he tapped a finger on it, making it swell even more. Then he lifted the syringe from where it lay on the ground beside him and injected a medley of drugs into his body. I was too fascinated to be scared, as I continued to stare at him. His eyes closed and his body went limp. All around us, filthy teenagers lay stoned amongst a mess of mud and used needles. A girl with wild hair staggered towards us. Suddenly I felt vulnerable. I had no right to be in their space to witness their degradation. I couldn't guess how long I'd been standing there. With a heart hammering against my ribcage, I strode out of Needle Park, a place I would never go back to again.

We moved on to the picturesque lanes of the *Altstadt*. In sharp contrast to the desperation and ugliness of Needle Park, this historical heart of the city was charming and atmospheric. In the centre of the old town, the Limat River was lined on both sides by pedestrian-only cobbled streets. A cornucopia of little buildings made up of homes, shops, restaurants and bars, were dotted along the winding alleys. Turrets, towers and castles reflected the medieval history of this quaint and authentic area, known for its shopping by day and nightlife after dark.

Over dinner, we hatched our plans for skiing. Since we would only have one full day free before our shuttle to Amsterdam, we decided to go on a day trip to the closest resort, Flumserberg, the following day. Then, once we had returned from the quick commute to Holland, we would go further afield to a bigger ski area for the two or three nights that remained, before we were to return to Johannesburg at the end of the ten-day trip.

Whatever we had planned, I knew it would be fun due to the fact that Denzil, our captain, was part of this group. His reputation as possibly one of the most mischievous people in the airline was a cloak he wore shamelessly. Notwithstanding this fact, he was also one of the most highly regarded pilots. And he was a great skier. The other person who would ensure that we laughed a lot, was Geoff Birchall, with his inclination for practical jokes. Also a highly regarded pilot. Not such a good skier.

Early the next morning, we set off by train for the ninety-minute journey. Some of us had come prepared and were kitted out in full ski regalia. Others, who it had to be said displayed a keen sense of adventure, arrived in jeans and airline-issue raincoats, which they intended wearing back-to-front in order to minimise the effects of the wind and snow, Geoff being one of these. Not that they aspired to gather too much speed on the downhills, as they had never skied before. The scary part was that they were expecting us to teach them.

Ski boots, in those days, were designed by despots to be used as objects of torture in countries with a total lack of human rights. It's a mystery how they found their way from torture chambers to ski slopes under the guise of recreation.

Armed with skis and poles, and with frozen feet mangled in these ill-fitting snow shoes, we ascended the Alps with the zeal of martyrs. After a brief introductory lesson on the nursery slopes with those of us who had skied before acting as instructors, we set off for higher ground, dragging the two uninitiated skiers up the T-bars with us. That alone had its challenges and took up most of the morning. We put them together on the first T-bar, with the following instructions,

'Do not sit down or stick your bottom out. Stand upright, knees slightly flexed, upper body leaning slightly towards your partner, weight on your skis with the bar resting on the lower part of your buttocks.' Simple. The fact that the one chap measured 6ft 4in and the other 4ft 6in was a crucial factor in their failure. Allow me to flirt with the truth here – the discrepancy in their height might not have been as severe, but it certainly was an element that contributed to the same result. The infuriated lift operator did not share in our mirth. In fact, I don't think he saw the funny side at all. I have to confess, I felt slightly vindicated at seeing Geoff Birchall tumble off the T-bar time and time again. Never again would he slap a sticker onto my back that said 'crew use only'.

A mixture of enthusiasm and determination finally got us to the top of the mountain. Now, the only challenge was getting back down. Fortunately, these two intrepid skiers were optimistic about their abilities. They needed no encouragement. With their navy blue raincoats billowing out behind them, they faced stoically downhill, with knees bent and skis in excess of two feet apart. With arms lifted high on either side and poles swinging dangerously, they proceeded to reach speeds of over Mach 6, yelling in their best German, '*Achtung*! Beginner. *Achtung*! Beginner,' as they cleaved a path toward the bottom of the slopes, with skiers on either side huddled in bewildered groups. Moses could not have done a better job parting the waters.

Unfortunately, they had not mastered the snowplough procedure, which meant that slowing down was not an option. Stopping was downright impossible. As they continued to gather speed, we sat hot on their heels, hopefully displaying slightly better technique.

Like the drop of an executioner's axe, they came to an uncontrolled stop at the bottom of the hill, where they ploughed into a group of unsuspecting children standing in line waiting for their ski school lesson to commence. I watched a confusion of red jackets and yellow bibs tumble like dominoes.

It's always funny until somebody gets hurt. Fortunately, or more likely, miraculously in this instance, nobody got hurt. The downside of this was that these two clowns interpreted the experience as being a success and were all geared up for a repetition. I suggested lunch instead.

It's never a good idea to have a few beers at lunchtime and then clip skis onto your feet. It's especially dumb when overconfident, inexperienced skiers in raincoats attempt this. Our final journey down the mountain after a last après ski drink was probably the most unprofessional version of skiing ever witnessed at Flumserberg. The eight of us lined up in the waning late afternoon light, ready to embark on a downhill race, imbued with the confidence only liquor can instil.

It was carnage. And this was before we even managed to get started. Les, the co-pilot, on the outside edge, leaned hard against Lynne who was standing next to him and pushed her over with such force that the entire row of us collapsed in a heap. This seemed like the funniest thing that had ever happened to us. We lay on the snow with arms outstretched convulsed with laughter, as Teutonic skiers took a wide berth around us on their final leg home. They thought we didn't understand what '*Scheisse*' and '*Arschloch*' meant. Finally we managed to gather ourselves together, readjust goggles, dust off the clumps of snow and form a line again.

Things deteriorated further. Denzil had a knack of skiing up right behind you and quickly inserting the tip of his ski pole into the back of your binding, causing it to unclip. This left you on a downhill race with one ski on, while your boot on the other foot gathered momentum rapidly as it tried to keep pace. We didn't get far in this fashion. A detritus of one-legged skiers lay scattered across the slope. I saw the evil glint in Denzil's eye as he approached a very German-looking skier, pole outstretched, poised for attack. I had a feeling this would not end well, so I launched myself into the path of the offending pole and managed to knock it off course. Just in time. The German continued, oblivious to the foiled attack while I gave myself a metaphorical pat on the back.

If there is a God, he was looking after us that day. We all made it down the mountain relatively unscathed and we even managed to make it all the way back to Zurich.

The shuttle to Amsterdam the next day was uneventful. But it was clear that the airline management had a very nasty collective streak. I have no doubt they put in these day trips just to make sure we didn't have too much fun. It entailed getting up in the very early hours of the morning, which in the middle of winter was no easy feat, schlepping out to the airport by bus and completing the one-hour journey as working crew. After a couple of hours at the destination, we would repeat this sequence in reverse. There was never really enough time at the end location to go into town to explore, although on occasion we did attempt a quick tour of the city, but the rush against time detracted from the enjoyment of experiencing a new place. I accepted that these mid-layover shuttles were a small price to pay for the pleasure of about seven full days of skiing. It was also a good opportunity for catching up on lost sleep.

Back in Zurich, we gathered at the concierge's desk to finalise plans for the next skiing trip. This was going to be the fun part, as we could look forward to a total of three solid days on the slopes – a mini-holiday, as it were. There was only one problem. It was December, just before Christmas. We were not the only ones who were keen to go skiing. Every resort the porter tried on our behalf was full. Of course, he could have been lying to us, trying to curtail our joie de vivre, as most of his countrymen had done their utmost to. But somehow I believed him.

Eventually he released the receiver from his ear, clasped his hand over the speaker and turned to us with what vaguely resembled a smile. Then he said something that echoed the sound of a large man clearing his throat, 'Melchsee-Frutt.' He had found a place for us to stay. In a combination of his best English and my best German, we established that this was not going to be five-star accommodation such as the Zurich Hilton. In fact, it was going be a lot less salubrious. The only thing they could offer us was what was known as laager accommodation, which comprised a small room with two sets of bunks on either side, each with a row of five sleeping-bags spread out on the mattresses. Talk about up close and personal. If we didn't know each other well before, we were certainly going to get to know each other intimately on this trip.

As one person, we replied, '*Gut. Danke.*'

That's what made air crew so refreshing to be around. No-one hesitated at trading the luxury of a five-star hotel for the squalor of shared bunk beds in a village with an unpronounceable name.

There was only one proviso. We insisted that the two intrepid skiers invested in proper ski jackets.

Posing in the cockpit on my first flight.

The 'Fluffy'.

Making announcements on board.

Touching up the 'lippie' in the loo.

Taking a break.

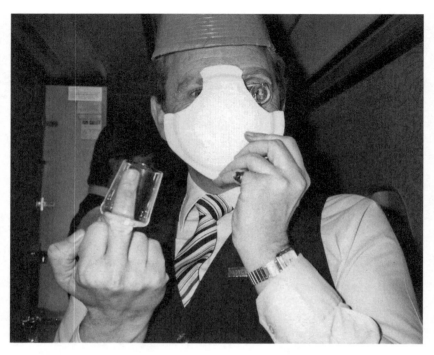

This is what we did with broken crockery on board!

London in the punk era.

Ditching practice in the pool during emergency training.

Wimbledon.

Boat trip to Coconut Island, Mauritius.

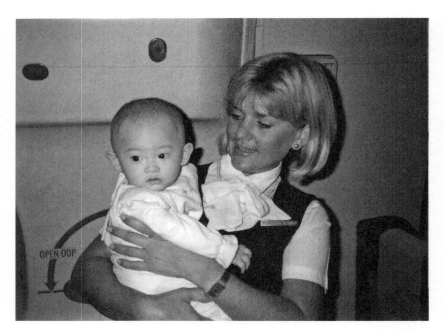

An adorable little passenger!

The floating restaurant in Hong Kong.

Snake Alley, Taipei.

Me and my mum in a tuk tuk in Bangkok.

The pool at Ilha do Sal.

New Year's Day on Ilha do Sal.

Skiing in Arosa.

Feeding the pigeons in Venice.

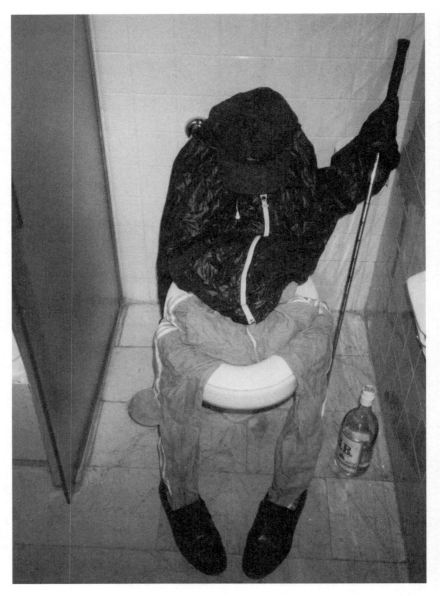

Shenanigans in Madrid after stealing the captain's room key.

The French Open tennis tournament.

Monaco.

Rottnest Island, Perth.

Running with the bulls in Sanguesa.

In front of Raffles Hotel, Singapore.

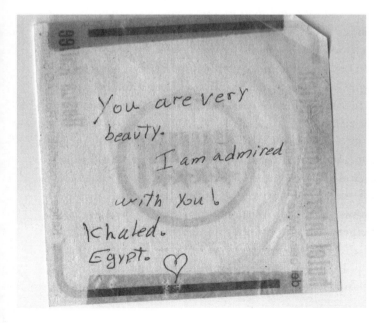

A note from a passenger.

9

LIVING IT UP IN LISBON

I'd never been to Lisbon before. But once again, in order to reach this agreeable destination, I first had to get the flight out of the way.

Everybody has heard of the mile-high club. Most people aspire to become a member of this club, which is harder to get into than Groucho's. Not because it's exclusive, but because it's almost physically impossible. What they don't realise is that it's a lot sleazier, too.

I've never been able to fathom the attraction of getting naked in a cubicle the size of a spittoon, only with a lot more germs. And a lot less space. Give me a public portaloo any day.

Inside every toilet on any aeroplane is an amber light. You will always find an accompanying instruction: 'Push in case of an emergency.' If you should suffer the misfortune of having a heart attack in the loo, you should push this amber button. You could also be forgiven for pushing this button if, due to the vacuum created by flushing the toilet, you found your rear end firmly attached to the toilet seat with absolutely no chance of dislodging it without outside intervention. This might also be considered an emergency. Pushing the amber button on either of these occasions would result in an orange light igniting on the outside of the toilet cubicle door, as well as at the crew station within that section of the plane. There would be an accompanying audible alert to make sure it did not go unnoticed. At least one crew member would then rush to the said restroom and enquire through the door what the problem was. In the case of the rear end stuck to the toilet seat, the crew member would zip off to the galley and return with a stainless-steel serving spoon to be used to prise the offending body part from the bowl. The exact procedure I shall leave to your imagination. Due to the fact that all metal cutlery nowadays has been replaced with plastic, they've had to modify the toilets.

However, on occasion, this orange light can also be pushed inadvertently, with absolutely no intention of calling the services of a member of the crew. In fact, I could say with a large degree of certainty, that the objective in this amorous instance would be to get in and out of the loo in record time, without being observed at all.

Such was the case on this particular Lisbon flight. No sooner had we taken off and the seatbelt lights extinguished, when there was a rhythmic ding-dong sound, combined with an on-and-off flashing light from the panel at the crew station next to the galley. The older and wiser crew knew that this signified one thing only – and it was not an emergency.

'Come,' they said as they led us to the offending toilet door.

In her sweetest voice, Stella asked, 'Can I help you? What's wrong?' There was no verbal response, but the light stopped flashing immediately.

Then a man's voice, 'No problem. Thank you.'

That was our cue to hang around noiselessly opposite the door. We heard stifled giggles and a lot of shuffling about. Finally, the door opened and a man and woman gasped at the five of us staring into their flushed faces. Busted! We continued gloating as they did the walk of shame down the aisle to their seats. I wondered if that was the kind of story they would tell their grandchildren one day.

I've never been able to figure out if the Portuguese are an extremely virile nation, or if it is simply due to their Catholic orientation, but something fed their lust on that particular flight. It might have been the in-flight vibrations, or the result of extreme turbulence. Either way, it wasn't something I expected to encounter in business class.

During the pre-take-off drinks service, I had noticed an attractive, olive-skinned gentleman sitting in the middle section of the last row of business class, against the bulkhead. He was in the aisle seat, F, on the starboard side of the plane. A woman was seated in the same row as him, but at the opposite end. She was in the aisle seat, D, on the portside. There was an empty seat between them. They were strangers to one another. They kept to themselves, both sitting silently through the start of the dinner service. Both consumed a fair amount of alcohol during the meal and I noticed that they had started up a conversation by the time we came to serving cheese and biscuits. Both asked for liberal measures of port. By now, she had moved into the previously empty seat between them. After dinner, they continued to order quite a few more drinks. I thought no more of it.

Once the service had been concluded, duty-free items sold and the lights put out for what was going to be a short night, those of us on first shift took up our customary positions on the metal bins in the galley. I was struggling with a crossword, others were reading magazines and the more conscientious amongst us were traipsing up and down the aisles offering drinks to those poor passengers too uncomfortable to sleep.

Disturbing our night vigil, Pieter burst into the galley, 'Jesus, Dolls, come and check this out!' He led us to that same back row of business class, where our attractive gentleman was now sitting, writhing in his seat, head thrown back, mouth agape and if I could have seen in the dim light, I'm sure his eyes would have been glazed over. Lying across the two empty seats, under the scanty disguise of a thin blanket, was the woman. Needless to say, her feet were at the opposite end of his crotch.

Pieter was none-too-gentle as he shook her by the legs until she finally sat up. Her hair was wild, her clothes dishevelled and her eyes bleary. 'Would you like something to drink?' he asked, with three of us lined up behind him, peering at her. That was one way of putting a stop to public indecency.

Now there is another walk of shame on an aircraft, which pertains to crew and not passengers. It is of a different nature altogether, but no less humiliating. So, I've told you about those lovely little hard bunks at the back of the plane in the crew rest, where we escaped from fornicating passengers. The bunks might have been hard, but not nearly as hard as stepping out into an aisle lined with passengers in the full glare of cabin lights when caught in a compromised position. I had been on duty for the first half of the rest period on this flight, which meant that I was afforded the luxury of putting my feet up for the second half (whoopee, an entire two-hour rest). The idea was that one of the crew members on duty would surreptitiously sneak to one of the loos – generally the one hidden in the very back corner of the plane – and, using a nail file or the tip of a pen, slide the latch across to read 'Occupied'. This person would then go to the entrance of the crew rest and vigorously shake every resting person's feet to wake them. This was all meant to happen well before the cabin lights were switched on, and passengers flooded the aisles, vanity bags the size of the *Titanic* under their arms, in a race to reach the ablutions, which they then hogged with unashamed selfishness.

Now, whether on that particular morning I had simply been too far in the depths of subconscious sex-inspired REM dreams as a direct result of the concupiscent behaviour of our guests, or whether the crew had colluded and intentionally omitted to ensure that I was awake, I did not know. But the consequences were the same. It was the noise that woke me. Flushing toilets, banging trolleys, loud voices. I was instantly on my feet, having fallen from the top bunk in blind panic. Oh fuckety-fuck. I grabbed my handbag and stepped beyond the flimsy curtain into a wall of musty-smelling bodies and lights brighter than the entire solar system.

I looked to the left. An endless queue. I looked to the right. Another queue, which stretched to beyond infinity. I had no option. I stepped out of the crew rest, with make-up smeared across my face. I could feel my eyelashes clustered together, as if I'd fallen asleep on a toffee apple. My hair was wilder than Robert Plant's from Led Zeppelin. I hung my head and avoided eye contact, as I ploughed through the throng of people, headed toward the nearest WC. Surely passengers would be polite under the circumstances. They wanted their breakfast, after all. Not a chance. They elbowed me out of the way, as I tried to get to the front of the queue. I looked up as Pieter called my name and mouthed at me, 'Back left.' Ah, great, he'd sealed that one off for me. There was only one problem; it was at the other end of the plane. Head down. Push. Shove. Elbow. Curse. Finally, I got there. I wriggled to the very front of the line, pulled an emery board out of the pouch of my handbag and slid the little lock to the open position. The vocabulary that filtered through the gap under the door was enlightening, to say the least. On the plus side, once I emerged from the restroom, they didn't recognise the new me, so I was safe. One woman did see through my make-over and actually asked if there was a magician in that loo, or if the water in the toilet taps came from Lourdes. I couldn't quite decide whether to smile at her or hit her.

When finally I was able to show my face in public, the breakfast service was already under way. I took over from the galley slave, who had stood in for me while I was reassembling myself. When we reached the couple in the back row of business class, I was delighted to see that their embarrassment was off the scale compared to mine earlier, albeit for different reasons. They had resumed their original seats at opposite ends of the row and determinedly avoided eye contact both with one another and the crew. It was as if they had never met. I cannot deny it gave me great pleasure going up to them both and asking, 'Did you have a good night? Please would you fold your own blanket.'

From the minute we touched down, I knew I was going to adore Lisbon and looked forward to getting to know it. The city is made up of hills, which all seemed to be covered in a kaleidoscope of white buildings with terracotta rooftops. I'd never seen streets so elegant, with mosaic patterns running the full length of each and every one. I grew to love its café culture and soulful Fado music. Despite the fact that it is spread across seven hills, it's small enough to be explored in just a few days. Walking up and down the hilly, cobbled streets enabled me to get a real feel for this charming maritime city. Lisbon is built around the point where the Atlantic Ocean and the Tagus River meet, so it exudes activity and energy. One of Lisbon's claims to fame is that it is the largest westernmost city of continental Europe.

The ambience is laid-back as people walk along the swirling black and white tiles in the main square, known as Rossio. This is the bosom of the city where, at any time of the day or night, you are likely to find an elderly shoeshine man soliciting business. Coffee shops and cafés are dotted all along the perimeter of the square. Men gather in groups, with blazers fashionably draped over their shoulders.

Walking along the narrow, medieval streets of the Alfama for the first time, was a novel experience. We even hopped onto an old wooden tram, as it wended its way along the cobbles. I found the area charming, despite the fact that it was slightly dilapidated. It felt more like a long-forgotten village within a city. I inhaled the atmosphere and found it captivating. It was like stepping back in time, as I watched century-old iron funiculars lurch and rumble as they ferried people to scenic points across the city. I knew that I would always come back to this part of town, with its picturesque pastel-coloured buildings and tiny doorways.

Lisbon is a city with soul. It encourages an insatiable appetite for long dinners and coffee breaks. Not that we ever needed much encouragement. Especially since the Portuguese food was robust, rather than refined. A good match for air crew, then.

I had seventeen glorious days to look forward to in this beguiling city. Somewhere in-between, there would be a shuttle to another European capital but, in the meantime, I was going to enjoy the first free week.

Lisbon was a favourite amongst the crew, principally due to its relaxed feel and attitude towards food. Air crew are creatures of habit. We met in the mornings for breakfast at the Green Door, followed by drinks in the evening at the Stone Church and culminating with dinner at the Chicken House. This was all fine once you knew your way around the city, but for a first-timer it was tough because every door was green, many pubs were converted old churches and just about every second restaurant's speciality was rotisserie chicken. It didn't get you anything more than a puzzled frown when you enquired about these venues by these names at the porter's desk. Yet, somehow, they became known and we were always likely to bump into fellow crew members at any of these three well-frequented joints.

The Chicken House turned out to be an unpretentious, well-patronised local haunt. The tables were adorned with nothing more than thin white paper cloths and greasy salt-and-pepper cellars. We drank wine from stubby glasses. White tiles with rich swirly yellow and blue designs covered the walls. It was not the decor that testified to the success of this restaurant – it was the mixture of heady aromas that fought for rank. A combination of intoxicating, piquant cooking smells, so pungent they were almost tangible, filled the air in the dingy place. Baskets of fresh crusty bread were thrust on the table, followed by large platters of French fries and bowls of heavily scented garlic beans. Waiters placed a white plate, with an entire half of a perfectly grilled chicken, in front of everyone. This was not a place where you were offered the liberty of choice. No á la carte and certainly not nouvelle cuisine.

On my first night in Lisbon, I had a taste of the latter two haunts. After Sagres beers at the Stone Church and vinho verde at the Chicken House, we moved on to the square with its heaving nightlife. Young people and old, some well-dressed and others casual, milled around in timeworn manner and tradition. They avoided the beggars, mostly unkempt mothers cradling deformed babies, the result of desperate women who mutilated their infants in order to forge a living out of begging on the streets. Shoeshiners sat on little stools as they polished the footwear of elegant gentlemen. I was introduced to a fascinating feature of Portuguese drinking culture, which was labelled by the crew as a 'hole in the wall'. A multitude of shot glasses, each containing a well-pickled, alcoholic cherry, were lined up on a counter in a small recessed area in a building. When you bought a glass, the barman filled it with a ruby liquid. They became known in airline-speak as 'cherry bombs'.

As if this was not enough, somebody always ordered a string of these drinks for everyone in our group and the 'shpit pipsh competish' would commence. So, on my introductory night, I was handed my shot and we all lined up in front of the unassuming little bar. I eyed the small glass of purple liquid and wondered how I was going to get away with pretending to drink this potent concoction. First of all, I had a very healthy respect for liqueurs. You didn't mess with them. In my experience, they always came back to hit you hard on the head. And secondly, I couldn't abide sweet drinks. I was still looking around for an avenue of escape, also known as cheating, when someone gave the signal. I panicked – there was no getting out of it. I was going to be forced to swallow. Blocking my nose with a thumb and forefinger, I downed the sickly sweet liqueur. It tasted like a mixture of Kool Aid and kerosene. I nibbled the flesh of the cherry and then proceeded to spit the pip as far as I possibly could. On either side of me, my teammates did the same. I was astonished at the fierce competitive spirit with which everyone participated, as they elbowed one another and pushed and shoved to get an advantage. The banter was incessant. This was clearly all about winning. Like golfers marking their balls as they flew across the fairway, everyone stormed forwards toward the end line to ensure there would be no dodgy judgement as to whose pip had travelled the furthest.

A young American chap in cut-off jeans and flip flops, was watching us. 'Hey, y'all, do it again. I'll be the judge this time,' he drawled in a southern American accent. Oh God, I thought, I was going to have to swallow another entire glass of liqueur. Three similarly dressed guys joined him. I had an idea – I'd do anything to avoid more cherry bombs – and suggested a team duel. As there were four of them, we would choose our four best spitters to compete. This left me securely off the hook.

It took at least twenty minutes to establish the procedure and rules. By this time, we were all firm friends. I'm not sure if it was due to the male testosterone, or the cutthroat rival instinct that called for the challenge to be repeated over and over. I suspect it was more likely due to the fact that they had all acquired an appetite for the revoltingly sweet drinks by that stage. The competition yielded no winners or losers – just a lot of drunken hugging, before the Yanks went off in search of new friends.

There was more spit on those cobbles than shoe polish by the end of the evening.

We returned to our luxury five-star Sheraton hotel in high spirits, reluctant to call an end to the evening. Leaving a baby grand piano in the foyer of a hotel that housed a variety of air crew was extremely short-sighted of the management.

The infamous captain Denzil walked up to the piano without a second's hesitation and opened the lid, revealing a polished keyboard. This was the cue for the co-pilot, Mike, never known for being reticent, to drape himself on top of the instrument, where he unbuttoned his shirt and assumed what he felt was a seductive pose. A sing-a-long ensued. Due to the lateness of the hour, we managed to get away with it for at least five seconds before security hauled us all out of the area. This resulted in de-camping to somebody's bedroom.

Girls and guys sprawled across beds and chairs. Somebody opened the mini-bar. Someone else suggested a game of 'feathers'. Nobody objected. We stripped a sheet off one of the beds, elicited a feather from a down pillow and formed a circle on the floor. Each person took hold of an edge of the perimeter of the bed linen with both hands, until it was stretched to maximum capacity in a haphazard round shape. The feather was placed in the centre of the taut sheet and everyone started blowing furiously. The objective of the exercise was to get the feather to flutter off the sheet and either onto or close to a person. It is at this point where the game resembled strip poker. As the contest got under way, more and more items of clothing littered the floor. From time to time, I wiped saliva that didn't belong to me off my face. Finally, due to some overzealous blowing, which could have been construed as cheating, the game was abandoned.

But this did not signify the end of the party. Artie turned up the music and poured more drinks. This was clearly headed for a 'One tequila, two tequila … where did my pants go?' type of gathering. Things rapidly degenerated. At some stage of the evening, I saw Denzil sidle up to the senior bag and overheard him slur, 'Hilda, would you consider performing a bit of fellatio?'

To which she replied without missing a beat, 'Oh God no, Captain. I don't do opera at all!'

That has to be the cleverest line in the book. Unless of course, she'd had cause to use it before. For all I knew, this might well have been a regular request at airline parties. At least I knew I had my answer ready should that invitation ever come my way in the future.

It was at this point that I decided to make my escape. I was nowhere near in the same league as these hardened drinkers. I snuck out of the room like a mouse. Although, if I'd announced my departure with a brass band, it might still have gone unnoticed, such was the comatose state of most of the revellers.

As custom dictated, we all met up at the Green Door for breakfast the next morning. If there is one word that has no place in the vocabulary of air crew, it has to be 'hangover'. Looking every inch as glamorous as if they were about to embark on a flight, everyone sat down at the breakfast counter and ordered the typical continental breakfast. This generally consisted of toast with jam, cheese or butter, but always included a pastry, in particular the heavenly *pastal de nata*, a light, custard-filled pastry with a hint of cinnamon.

Instead of experiencing embarrassment or remorse inspired by the memories of the previous evening, much to my surprise the entire event was rehashed and relived in a full-blown post-mortem. Nursing a slight sense of alcohol-induced nausea and a touch of shame, I almost felt like an intruder.

The plan was to take the train to a quaint little fishing village nearby called Cascais. Lisbon provides a great base from which to explore the natural beauty of the surrounding areas, historic towns and glorious sandy beaches, all just a day trip away.

Headed for the Cais do Sodre station, we ambled down the Avenida da Liberdade, the Portuguese equivalent of the Champs Elysées. This is the main road in Lisbon, which was built in the nineteenth century and was, in fact, fashioned in the style of the famous French boulevard. This elegant avenue is more than 300ft wide and is lined with fountains and café tables, shaded by trees. The pavement is decorated with a swirl of abstract patterns, one of the endearing hallmarks of Portugal's streets.

The forty-five-minute train ride ran all along the coast, passing towns romantically called Belém, Oeiras, Carcavelos and Estoril, before finally reaching the historic fishing port of Cascais on the very western edge.

What a pretty little town! It positively oozed sophistication and class. I could see right away that this place was home to the rich and famous. I wasn't wrong because I discovered that, during the nineteenth century, this elegant town had become the summer retreat for the Portuguese nobility and the high society of Europe. As far as I looked along the coast, I glimpsed sandy beaches and turquoise seas. Huge rocky outcrops jutted into the water. There were sun loungers and people, and yachts with white sails whimsically unfurled bobbed in the bays or cut across the ocean. The languid atmosphere, as well as the natural beauty of the place, wriggled its way into my soul and I knew then and there that I would always come back to Cascais. The other side was an equally fascinating collection of white buildings, with the traditional terracotta-coloured roofs. As we walked around the cobbled streets, I was fascinated by the architecture and how traditional buildings, grand houses, recreational venues and beautiful parks all blended together. Tall palm trees lined the swirly-patterned pavements. In contrast to the serenity of the coastal side, music, laughter and chatter spilled out of the many restaurants and bars, giving us an almost unlimited choice of entertainment options.

The restaurant we went to was slightly out of town, in a residential area. The Ginginia Transmontana was a tiny, family-run enterprise. It is possibly the quirkiest eating-house I have ever been to. The walls and roof were adorned with items ranging from a football to ballet shoes, and clocks to farming implements. It was crowded to the point of discomfort, but the food, which was served on roof tiles, was outstanding. It was broad daylight when we entered and dusk when we left.

Next stop had to be sundowners at the Albatroz Hotel. En route, however, we lost one of our party, Karl, who had ducked into a touristy shop to buy two fold-up beach chairs. The reason he decided to buy these obscure items, on this specific day, in this particular resort town, has never been ascertained. One can only assume that alcohol played a role in his decision-making.

The charming boutique hotel was a place of true glamour that hovered just above the ocean, away from traffic and the hustle and bustle of the town centre. White umbrellas deflected the last rays of the setting sun. Loungers with ivory mattresses teased us from where they rested alongside the pool. As we sat on the terrace of the panoramic bar overlooking the bay of Cascais, I nibbled nuts from a white porcelain bowl and sipped crisp *vinho verde* from a long-stemmed glass. In the fading light, with the smell of the sea in my nostrils and the sound of the waves lapping at the rocks beneath us, I closed my eyes, relaxed into the soft, white sofa and indulged in the magic of the place. I wondered briefly if I might have died and gone to heaven.

All too soon it was time to go. We paid our bill and headed to the station for the return journey. Waiting on the platform was our friend Karl, who by this stage had acquired a further collapsible lounger. He was delighted to see us and opened up the chairs, inviting us to join him as he set them out in a circle on the platform. Somebody hauled two cans of Sagres out of a rucksack. The beers got passed around, with absolutely no concern for picking up any unmentionable social diseases. In this fashion, we relaxed and waited for the train. Our fellow commuters were forced to take a wide berth around us. The fact that they were not on holiday, but simply trying to get home after a long day at work, did not endear us to them. They didn't intimidate us. We interpreted their hostile glances as envy.

The following days brought further trips to places such as the picturesque town of Óbidos. According to history, it was given to Queen Isabel, in the thirteenth century, as a gift by her husband King Denis simply because she had marvelled at its beauty. Apparently, for centuries after, the various incumbent kings of Portugal upheld the tradition of presenting the quaint little town to their bride queens. This ancient walled city is located on a hillside and offers magnificent views of the Estremadura area, with a medieval castle as its main attraction. We walked the entire perimeter of the town along the wall, which presented many opportunities for tripping on the uneven surfaces, further endangering our lives due to a complete absence of safety railings. However, the view over the terracotta-tiled roofs and white-painted houses was worth the risk.

On another day, we visited Portugal's most famous fishing village, Nazare. It was like stepping back in time, as we watched old women along the seafront drying shimmering loads of fish, in the sun, on wooden racks lined with netting. They were dressed completely in black and suspicious of posing for photographs. Colourful wooden fishing boats evoked a sense of fishermen in the Phoenician times. The vessels were narrow, with curved prows, some of which still had a watchful eye painted on them to look out for shoals and storms. Many had lamps dangling from them, enabling the men to fish after sunset.

Another unique tradition we encountered was that of fisherwomen dressed in colourful layers of skirts. The seven layers of fabric had mythical and magical attributions, such as representing the days of the week, colours of the rainbow, as well as the seven waves in a set. A further theory is that the fishwives of old used to wait on the cold, wet and windy beaches for their men to return, and they put on multiple layers to keep themselves warm. Either way, it was refreshing to see these brightly coloured petticoats flutter along the streets and beaches, after the drab, black garb of the older and more serious women.

Nazare used to be known primarily for its fishing and its food. However, in recent years it has gained fame as one of the most important places for big-wave surfing, attracting surfers from all over the world with its monster waves. This seaside town currently holds the record of a 100ft wave surfed by a now world-famous Hawaiian, Garrett McNamara.

Back in Lisbon, it was the evening before our shuttle to Rome the following day. This meant an early morning wake-up call, around five. Lizzy and I snuck away from dinner before the rest of the gang and, with their complicity, managed to solicit a duplicate key to Denzil's room from an unsuspecting receptionist. Once inside, we located the regulation sewing kit in the bathroom and set to work stitching up the sleeves and legs of the captain's uniform. We worked like Santa's elves, threading needles, stitching and tying knots until we were satisfied that we had sealed off all entry or exit of hands and feet. In hindsight, that was a little like being a cyber hacker;

all we could find pleasure in was imagining his consternation at 5 a.m., as, like the rest of us, he probably would've only allowed himself the bare minimum time to get ready. It was sad that none of us would actually be there to witness his panic. But seeing him board the crew bus fifteen minutes late the following morning, with white threads dangling from his uniform sleeves, was enough compensation.

10

MADNESS IN MADRID

The one thing that I associate with Madrid flights is garlic. Not lovely little strings of garlic artfully plaited together. Nor the enticing aroma of this potent bulb during cooking. I'm not fooled by the innocent papery skin or the pale yellowish flesh within each individual clove. As my mother used to say, 'Appearance isn't everything.' Just like its cousin, the onion, it's been put upon this earth to deceive us. What is garlic anyway? A herb? A spice? Or a vegetable? Or is it simply another one of God's jokes, tricking us into eating something that looks and tastes so good, yet once you've ingested it, you may as well go into self-imposed exile on a desert island.

Which is exactly what I wished the entire embarking crew had done on the morning I arrived at Barajas Airport on my first trip to Madrid. We landed at around five in the morning, bone-weary as always after the eleven-ish-hour flight. In fact, I could have been conned into believing that I had walked the full distance from Johannesburg to the Spanish capital. The only thing that kept me on my feet was the mental image of arriving at my five-star hotel, with its firm mattress and delicately scented bed linen. And the supposition that I could relax, in a crumpled heap, on the hour-long bus journey between the airport and the hotel.

The 'fresh' crew boarded the plane, ready for the handover in preparation for their shuttle to Paris or some other equally exotic European destination. Now, I have to remind you that they had already spent three days indulging in the traditional, full-flavoured Iberian fare. Let's face it, tapas would not be tapas without at least 14kg of garlic per 100g of edible material.

Ah! Eau de aeroplane. I am the first one to admit that a jumbo jet carrying around 270 passengers and fourteen crew members after a long-haul intercontinental flight does not exactly smell like a freshly picked bunch of sweetpeas – more like the armpit of an unwashed coal miner – but it's not often that the incumbent crew could compete with this. I was not prepared for the nasal onslaught that their arrival inflicted upon us. The already contaminated air was immediately filled with enough stale garlic to prise the feathers off a rooster's tail. One by one, we hit the deck like a row of skittles in a bowling alley, as we were greeted by our foul-smelling colleagues. A blue haze filled the cabin. A female passenger, sitting in the row of seats just opposite the crew jump seat, searched frantically through her bag and finally pulled out the slumber shades she had been given the night before. I assumed she wanted to try and sleep through the noisy handover. I was wrong. Instead of slipping them over her eyes, her fingers gripped the fabric as she pulled it firmly over her nose. This accomplished, she then gave the elegant hostess, who looked good but smelt bad, a reprehensible look. I could tell she didn't want to swap me for the new girl. She was probably the first passenger ever to feel this way. Ah well, you've got to take your compliments where you can. Who was I to question her motivation?

That gave me an idea. I grabbed the demo oxygen mask which I 'placed firmly over both nose and mouth whilst breathing normally' and gurgled hand-over instructions to my compatriot. Unfortunately, this made her laugh. My intention had not been for her to spew forth even more rank fumes. Now the lady passenger was cross with me, too. I winked an apology at her and turned around as I went in search of my cabin bag, which held my step-out shoes. The minute we got on board an aircraft, we exchanged these high heels for flat, comfortable cabin shoes. They generally looked and fitted like slippers. Not pretty, but comfortable. I typically waited until the very last minute before getting off the plane, to go through the painful saga of donning the glamorous, but uncomfortable step-outs. What I hadn't accounted for on this occasion, was that the king of practical jokes, my good old friend Geoff Birchall, was on the flight. Not only was he funny, but he had a good memory, too. He had not forgotten the T-bar saga on his skiing trip to Flumserberg. Revenge was what he was after.

I scratched around in my black leather bag, which held my pinafore, the less than fresh blouse and knickers I had worn when I started out the flight (we always changed in the mornings, after a stint in the crew rest, just before switching on the lights and serving breakfast), deodorant, perfume and a horde of make-up and hair repair kit. It should also have held a pair of elegant, high-heeled navy blue leather shoes. It held only one of these. I searched frantically for the missing shoe and cursed myself – how could I have been so stupid as to lose one? But I knew it couldn't have gone far. Well, it had obviously travelled 20,000 miles already, but it couldn't have gone any further than that. Not on its own. I scratched around the general area where I had left my bag, behind the last row of seats in economy class. We all shoved them there for quick access during the dark hours, when a mini makeover was sometimes required after a little finger surgery in the loos. Occasionally, we were so desperate for privacy on a flight that we locked ourselves in the dimly lit toilets. And then, out of sheer boredom, one sometimes sought out spots on one's face with the ferocity of a hunting dog on the trail of a pheasant. Not a blackhead survived this witch hunt. The result was an angry-looking, inflamed and patchy cheek or chin. This is where your on-board stash of lotions and potions came into their own.

The missing shoe continued to elude me. I was in a dilemma – it was completely forbidden to even consider appearing in public dressed in full uniform and, at the same time, wearing cabin flats. An offence so serious, it could result in dismissal. We had an image to protect, after all, and good legs were part of it.

Panic gripped at me while *tempus fugited*, as they say in Latin. The entire new crew was now on board and I could not spot a single one of my own colleagues left on the plane. Time to go. I shoved my well-worn flatties into the bag and donned the one glamorous high heel. I then grabbed my bags and hobbled down the aisle, holding my breath as I made my way towards the front of the plane, avoiding further injury to my olfactory senses. I couldn't decide which was worse – the consternation of running on one shoe-ed foot, or taking it slowly so as not to be too obvious. But I had to escape the garlic. I continued my lopsided journey, weaving between the seats, not daring to breathe. I didn't care that my face was turning blue at this stage – it was the lesser of two evils.

Just when I thought it was safe again, mainly because I had reached the point when I was about to faint from lack of oxygen, I drew a deep breath. Big mistake. As I stared into the murky eyes of the one and only customs official, I was yet again assaulted by the vile odour of fetid Allium sativum. Not only was it on his breath, I'm pretty sure I even glimpsed a speck of it lurking in the dark fibres of his not insubstantial moustache. I was beginning to wonder what had possessed me to voluntarily request this trip to Madrid. But in my defence, I hadn't known about the garlic.

By now, my survival instinct had completely overtaken my innate impulse toward sophistication, as I limped along like the Hunchback of Notre Dame. My unshod Achilles screamed in protest each time my stockinged foot hit the floor in see-saw fashion. At least there were no crew members to witness my humiliation ... for the time being. I did draw a few amused glances from passers-by, but my snarled response about showing sympathy for me, having snapped a tibialis anterior, was enough to make them wipe those smiles right off their faces. Swaying from side to side as first one heel clicked loudly on the tiles, and then alternated with the soundless tapping of a pointed, stockinged toe on the same surface, I knew I was rather conspicuous. With one leg a good few inches shorter than the other, I eyed up any potential size-six-wearing females in similar shoes, as I formulated a plan to push her over and nick the left one. Then run.

As I neared the baggage area, I spotted them. The entire crew was huddled together to witness my inelegant approach. Collusion was rife. Geoff hoisted my shoe up high, grinning. It was 2-1 to him. I snatched it from him and contemplated introducing the heel to his frontal lobe. Instead I said to him,

'Not funny. I had polio as a child and this brought back all those painful memories.' He looked mortified: 2 all.

We collected our suitcases and, with my shoe firmly back on my foot, traipsed to the coach where I sank deeply into the luxury of my leather seat. I lay back and inhaled the deliciously garlic-free atmosphere.

On arrival at the Eurobuilding Hotel, we queued up for our keys and meal allowance and then I took myself off to my room. I was not going to be coerced into a de-briefing drinks session this time. I wanted to grab a few hours of sleep, after which I intended to explore the unfamiliar city.

I had agreed to meet up with Annette, a hostie who had been on my initial intake into the airline. In the early days, we had both lived in Pretoria and shared a lift club whilst we were in training in Johannesburg. Our airline careers had developed in tandem, though we didn't see that much of each other once we moved to the international routes. It was good to be on the same flight and I was looking forward to our spending time together.

After a well-deserved rest, I made my way downstairs. Annette was already waiting in the foyer when I got out of the lift. I grabbed a map from the concierge, after he had boldly circled 'You are here', indicating the Eurobuilding Hotel which he pronounced with more guttural finesse than any self-respecting German would have been able to muster. Don't be misled by the spelling. It sounds something like a dog growling in a low pitch, 'Gggggggg ... urobuilding'.

We had four hours to familiarise ourselves with the city, before meeting the chaps in the hotel reception for dinner. So, off we went, trainers elegantly adorning our feet. Not. Well, I mean they adorned our feet, but were by no means elegant.

I found Madrid a seductive city of graceful boulevards and manicured parks. Even by day, there was an energy that shouted its message from the rooftops: this place knows how to live! I could just imagine the vibe at night. Unlike in Paris, where, despite my passable – if I may say so myself – French, I had never really felt welcome, Madrid embraced us with open arms. The experience was one of being absorbed into the bosom of this fervent culture. The colours were bright, the music was loud, the people were passionate. Simply by virtue of the fact that I was in Madrid, allowed me the indulgence of feeling that I was from Madrid. Actually, that's not my line – I think I heard that expression somewhere. But if nobody objects, I'm happy to claim it as my own.

Another thing about Madrid is its artistic pedigree, which can't be rivalled by many cities, boasting some of the finest art museums. I had done my research and I knew that the Prado was filled with home-grown talents such as Velázquez (endearingly pronounced Velathqueth) and Goya. While I was proud of myself for knowing this, I wasn't interested enough to actually visit the museum. A girl only has so much time to shop, after all.

We made our way to the main square, called the Plaza Mayor, with its bronze statue of King Philip III at the centre. The magnificent, symmetrical, red-brick building, with its many arches, was mostly made up of three-storey houses with little balconies looking out onto the square. I was overwhelmed by the imperial nature of the architecture. It certainly was fit for a king. A host of restaurants and cafés skirted the perimeter. We ambled along the periphery of the bustling tables. Everyone solicited our business, unashamedly. At first, we were flattered by the attention. We smiled and flirted in return, until we realised the fickle intent of these dark and handsome men. It was not about us at all; it was about getting bums in seats. Our bums into their seats. By the time the third waiter, dapperly dressed in black and white and solid as an oak, blocked our way, threatened us with a banderillo and practically forced us sit down, we capitulated. Well, that's the way I recall it. It had absolutely nothing to do with the fact that we were salivating for a drink.

There is something I will always remember about Spain and that is the flamboyant manner in which the Spaniards pour a gin and tonic, locally referred to as a 'gin-tonic'. The Dutch may take credit for having invented the gin (and I thank God every night in my prayers for this contribution from the Hollanders) and the Brits can have the kudos for the tonic, but it is the Spanish who elevated this elixir of life to an art level. Upon ordering said gin-tonic, the waiter reappeared and placed a glass resembling a fishbowl on a stem in front of each of us. But this was not just an empty glass; it was filled with ice cubes. Not a meagre two or three ice cubes, but about a 124. Perched on top of the cubes was a tantalising slice of lemon. The opaque flesh teased me from where it snuggled against the sliver of rind, the colour of a new moon. By this stage, I could have been mistaken for one of Pavlov's pets. Jesus (by now we'd learnt our waiter's name), pronounced in growling dog fashion, 'Gggggg … asus', returned a few seconds later with a tall, slim, cobalt-blue bottle and proceeded to pour from a great height directly onto the garnish. He was generous with the liquor. The tangy, aromatic infusion of the gin and the lemon brought a weakness to my knees that would have rendered me prostrate on the cobbled square, had I not been seated. There has clearly never been a market for tot measures in this country. I wondered where he intended to put the tonic. Not that I complained; that was his problem.

We spent a leisurely afternoon, chatting and sipping our way through those majestic drinks, indulging in the ambience of the square and the combined soporific effects of the sun and the alcohol. Finally it was time to haul ourselves out of our seats. Dragging our heels, we made our way back to our hotel with the name that sounded like an exercise in the clearing of one's nasal passages. When spoken like a true Spaniard, that is.

After a quick freshen-up in my room, and about a gallon of water to restore my equilibrium, I met the rest of the gang in the foyer of the hotel. It was time to experience Madrid by night!

The streets were thrumming with people. Apparently Madrid's obsession with nightlife is partly due to the climate – in the summer months, it is simply too hot to venture out before sundown. Hence the inception of the age-old tradition of the siesta. People only go out late in the evening and return in the early hours of the morning. The main attractions appeared to be tapas bars, cocktail bars, flamenco theatre, jazz lounges and live music. Revellers flocked in and out of many of these places. The real nightlife would only kick off after midnight, once the clubs opened. I was surprised to see young children running around, playing, while their parents gathered in groups, either in the parks or on the streets, drinking. Back home, this kind of behaviour would have led to the welfare authorities forcibly removing your children, in order to provide them with a more stable existence in an institutionalised environment. I knew which kids would be having more fun.

We entered a street-level bar which the captain, Posh Nigel, called 'The Hanging Ham'. There was a clue in there somewhere, which I missed. I pointed out to him, in my best

Spanish accent, that it was actually called 'Catha Gonthaleth'. I had mastered the lisp. In fact, between the guttural consonants and the penchant for what sounded like a speech impediment, I had quickly conquered the phonetics of the patois. I spoke the accent perfectly, without a trace of the language.

The bar was a dim, smoke-stained cavern, with enormous legs of cured ham hanging on metal hooks from the rafters. I couldn't help wondering how many human heads might have made contact with that meat, leaving behind a few tell-tale strands of hair. The walls and floors were tiled, the walls decorated with bright posters advertising impending bullfights. Upturned wine barrels served as rustic cocktail tables. For all its dinginess, it should have been sleazy but it wasn't. It exuded a romance of yesteryear. Behind the owner – an amiable-looking man with a sizeable moustache whose father had owned the pub before him, and his father before him, and his father before him (not an indisputable fact, based purely on intuition) – a row of Rioja bottles, covered in dust, fought for position amongst raffia-encased Chianti. Despite – or most likely due to – its completely informal atmosphere, the place was humming. We squeezed our way through to the counter, where we all stood, propping it up. Posh Nigel's philosophy in life was that you had to stand and drink. He was an ex-RAF man and seldom let anyone forget that.

Tapas are generally made from traditionally Mediterranean ingredients such as olive oil, our old friend the troublesome garlic, fish, seafood and pork. I sound as though I was totally familiar with tapas bars. In fact, I had been no closer to one than I had been to climbing Everest in flip-flops, until this day. But I slotted straight into 'tapear-ing' – the Spanish tradition of going from bar to bar for drinks and appetizers. In the early hours of the morning, when we made our way back to the hotel, the streets were no quieter. It was obvious that no matter how late you pounded the pavements in Madrid, you would never be walking alone.

There are few things in life more pleasurable than a comfortable bed when you are so tired that you have lost the will to live. We parted ways at the hotel's lifts and all agreed to touch base in the morning. We had one more day to explore the city, before our full-day shuttle to Brussels.

However, when I awoke to the sun blazing through my curtains the next morning, I decided to forgo any sightseeing and spend the day working on my suntan instead. There was a gorgeous penthouse pool at the hotel and, if I listened carefully, I could hear the sun loungers calling my name. I ordered a pot of coffee from room service. When my doorbell chimed a couple of minutes later, I opened the little slatted door that separated my bedroom from the main door in the small entrance hall. Another door on the side led into the bathroom. I opened the main door into the passage and stood aside to let in the stocky waiter. The brazen way in which he eyed me, as I stood in my hotel-issue waffle-weave gown, made me feel uneasy. He had dark hair on the back of his hands and I noticed a broad, gold wedding-band as he bent low and put the tray down on the dressing-table. I felt vulnerable being in such close proximity to him and was eager to get him out of my room, so I signed the slip of paper and handed him a few pesetas' tip. He thanked me, turned and walked through the door. I thought no more of it, poured my coffee and lay back on the bed to enjoy the strong Spanish blend. A short while later I got up, pulled out my bikini and started getting dressed for the pool. Heading for the bathroom, I yanked open the little slatted door whereupon the scurrilous waiter sprang up and bolted for the main door. I was too angry to be afraid. I lunged after him and shouted, but by the time I peered out of the main door he was out of sight. I could not believe this pervert had been crouched behind the door for at least twenty minutes, peeping through the slats as I got dressed. I was furious with him for such an invasion of my privacy, but I was more annoyed with myself for being so stupid.

When I met Annette at the pool half an hour later, I bombarded her with the horrors of my nasty little experience with the scopophiliac waiter. She was shocked and insisted that I report him to the hotel management right away. But I would never have been able to describe him; all I could remember were his hairy hands. Anyway, I'm a firm believer in not wasting time on negative energy. I had learnt a lesson and would be more vigilant in my future travels. The little country bumpkin from Bushbuck Ridge was growing up fast.

Lying at the pool, we discussed the fact that we would have four full days free after our commute to Brussels the following day, before we needed to board the flight back to Johannesburg. And so it happened that, three days later, we found ourselves on a trip to the Costa Brava. Somebody, somewhere had instilled in Annette the need to visit a town in the Catalonia region plumb on the Mediterranean called Lloret de Mar. I don't know what she had done to upset that friend. It turned out to be one of those slightly tacky budget holiday destinations. To say that I kept longing for my five-star hotel in an exclusive area of Madrid is an understatement.

At great expense, we had made our way back to the airport, where we had boarded a coach for a 236-hour un-air-conditioned journey via Vietnam to this seaside resort. Actually, we went via Barcelona; it just felt like Vietnam. On arrival in the former little fishing village, we hauled our bags over cobblestones to the building with the big, blue 'I' sign. They offered us a wealth of competitive accommodation to choose from. Our friendship at that stage was stretched thin. I gritted my teeth like a trapeze artiste without a safety net, as I tried to explain to Annette that just because it was popular didn't mean it was nice; it meant it was cheap. Did I mention that I was missing my five-star hotel back in Madrid?

I exaggerate. It was actually a very pretty place, with lovely beaches washed by crystal clear waters, just as the brochures would say. If there's one thing I was good at, it was always looking on the bright side of life. Oh, to be back in Madrid between my Egyptian cotton sheets!

We found an adequate place to stay, dropped our bags and went in search of transport. With our friendship and humour fully restored, Annette hired a Vespa and I settled for a bicycle. I had a very healthy respect for European drivers, deeply ingrained primarily due to an experience many years before on a Greek island where chickens, goats and motorcyclists received the same treatment from the local drivers: they were mown down indiscriminately if they weren't fast enough … or if they were on the road at all. I was happier pedalling away on the pavements.

We made our way to one of the many beaches. The sign said, 'Boadella Beach.' It looked lovely. The sand was thick and golden and it was surrounded by rocky outcrops, with lots of vegetation. We trundled down the narrow steps armed with beach towels and suntan oil. On the last step, I faltered. Before me, scattered like debris after a botched rocket-landing, was an assortment of naked human flesh – smooth, hairy, dark, light, protuberant, concave, asymmetrical, disproportionate and in some cases, downright cockeyed. We had stumbled upon a naturist's paradise. Not only were these nudists disseminated across an acre of flaxen sand, but some of them were actually roaming free. Now, I don't know how you feel about this, but in my innocent, early twenties, the sight of a crepe-skinned, sunburnt, potbellied octogenarian sporting a flaccid male organ of copulation flopping from side to side as he shuffled across the beach, an inane smile spread across his wrinkled face, filled me with abject horror. The world as I knew it had gone mad. This could never have happened in the insular, backwater community in which I had grown up. In all probability, it would have been illegal.

We found another beach, a family one this time, closer to the restaurants, shops and bars. As we were enjoying Fanta orange from frosted glasses, we noticed a large poster advertising a bullfight in the local arena. I could think of nothing worse. I was vehemently opposed to it. Yet, I felt compelled to see for myself what it was that this nation protected in the name of tradition. Certain things define the Spanish nation and sadly, bullfighting ranks up there right beside tapas, siestas and flamenco.

We arrived at the arena in time for the 7 p.m. start. All my years of playing Trivial Pursuit had finally paid off. I knew that the most expensive seats at a bullring were the ones in the shade. Budget dictated that we settled for the mid-priced tickets: the ones that started in the sun and ended in the shade. It also meant that we were slightly higher up and further away from the action.

A parade of bullfighters entered the ring. They strutted about in flamboyant costumes flashing sequins and beads of gold and silver. On their heads sat uniquely shaped hats – flat topped with round bulbs above each ear. These were elaborately embroidered and decorated. The jackets were short and appeared rigid, with heavy-looking brocade on the shoulders. Close-fitting tights, which extended to just below the knee, were tied with tasselled cords and decorated gaiters. On their feet were flat, ballerina slippers; in their hands, luxuriously embroidered capes. This spectacle gave a whole new meaning to the term 'dressed to kill'.

The mood was festive, as the matadors were introduced amidst much noise. I found myself swaying to the rhythm of Latin-American music. Eventually, a bull was let into the arena. The matadors disappeared discreetly except for one, who started tormenting the animal with various flashy dance moves involving a brightly coloured cape. I could cope with the teasing because, at that stage, the bullfighter seemed at greater risk of being gored or trampled. I didn't know that this was merely an opportunity for the matador to observe the bull's behaviour and quirks. But once the picador entered and started the unspeakable cruelty of stabbing the beast just behind the shoulder, I could no longer bear to watch. I covered my eyes with my hands as the animal lowered his head and horns slightly in his weakened state. The next stage saw three *banderilleros* planting yet more sharp sticks into the bull's shoulders. I peeked through my fingers, tears spilling down my cheeks. By now the bull was frothing at the mouth, agitated and angry, as he charged each of them randomly. In the final stage, the matador re-entered the ring with a red cape. I had always believed the colour was intended to anger the bull even more, but apparently the purpose was to mask its blood. With the traditional red cape, he continued to attract the bull in a series of dramatic passes as he arched his back and, looking impressive, stood on tiptoe. This wore the wretched animal down even more. It was also a means for the matador to display his domination of the bull, as he brought it dangerously close to his body. I could not bring myself to watch the final part of this display. It was barbaric. I could see that Annette felt the same as me. We left before the bull died.

There can't be many crueller forms of entertainment and it surprised me how this could be justified as sport by a sophisticated, developed nation. During the bullfighting season, which began in March and ended in October, every year an astonishing 24,000 bulls were killed in Spain. However, I'm delighted to learn that the Spaniards have finally seen reason. Over the past thirty years, bullrings have been closed down in the major Catalan towns, including Lloret de Mar. The Catalan parliament voted to outlaw it completely. Despite resistance from traditionalists, many bullrings were demolished after attempts to save them had failed. It certainly looks like the days of this horrific practice are numbered.

Supporters of the tradition have always held the opinion that bullfighting is an integral part of their national culture, an ancient ritual which demonstrates style, technique and courage. I am with those who oppose it as cowardly and sadistic. The torture, humiliation and ultimate killing of a bull amidst the self-promoting pomp and pageantry is inhumane and an outdated practice.

In my best Spanish, all I have to say is that it is a load of '*El toro* poo poo'.

11

PACKING FOR PERTH

One of the few places I hadn't been to was Australia, so I was delighted to find that I had been rostered for a seventeen-day Perth flight. It was almost going to be like decentralising – I would need to pack my entire wardrobe. It would also be a bit like home from home, as pretty much half of the entire white South African population had moved to Western Australia by that stage.

Seventeen days was a long time to be away; I was very happy that Lizzy was going to be with me. It sometimes happened that you could find yourself on a flight with nobody to hang out with, because some of the crew might have had friends or family at the destination that they were going to be visiting. Others could have had travel plans during the layover and some may have been couples – married couples, gay couples, or one half of the pair married and the other waiting her entire lifetime for him to leave his wife and family. There were a lot of those one–half-married couples in the airline and there was an unspoken code of conduct amongst the crew when it came to acceptance. These couples would do every single one of their flights together and would be known to everyone as X and Y, as if they were joined at the hip. After years of seeing them together, the combination of X and Y would just trip off your tongue. But then, out of the blue one day, the pilot's wife might decide to join him on a little sojourn and suddenly we would have X and Z to contend with. No matter how much you might have despised the captain in question and how tempting it could've been to drop him in it, the entire crew would have turned against you if you as much as contemplated that little act of sabotage.

On a short layover like London flights, it didn't matter at all if everyone else had plans or company as I would only have two or three days to amuse myself and, in a place like London, that would not be a challenge at all. But a seventeen-day flight could have posed a problem and been very lonely.

The nine-and-a-half-hour flight from Johannesburg to Perth proved to be mostly uneventful, save for the little incident with the lip balm.

Somewhere over the Indian Ocean, in the pitch-dark early hours of the morning, I was delivering a cup of tea to one of the boys in blue in the cockpit. He complained about the dry air and chapped lips. 'You wouldn't have a tube of lip balm for me, would you?' he asked.

I didn't hesitate, 'Sure. Of course I do. I'll just get it for you.'

Now, I blame my love of lipstick 100 per cent on my mother. As a young adult, she was forever pestering me to wear brighter lipstick. I favoured the more subtle, natural colours but between her and the airline, I finally relented and invested in mounds of shades, varying in colour from 'possibly-meeting-the-man-of-my-dreams-on-Friday-night' bright red DESIRE to 'oh-I'm-just-popping-to-Spar-but-I-might-bump-into-someone-I-know' pink INNOCENT.

Lipstick is a wonderful accessory and, if ever I was going to be banished to a remote island and was allowed to take only one item of make-up with me, I could without a nanosecond's hesitation say that my choice would be lipstick. If you, like me, are one of those unfortunate mortals not blessed with the bee-stung lips of Angelina Jolie, but bear a closer resemblance to Caspar the ghost, you would understand that I don't just like lipstick – I NEED lipstick. Without that splash of colour, my face is devoid of any definition and you could be forgiven for thinking that a tracheotomy had caused my voice to come from a hole somewhere in my throat. That's how invisible my naked lips are.

The problem is that lipstick only has a very brief lifespan, once it's been painted onto your kisser. I was permanently walking around with a tube of Estée Lauder wedged either somewhere in my bra or other parts of my underwear. This was especially applicable at any time that I was in an airline uniform, to avoid the possibility of being fired on the spot for a flaw in personal grooming.

Then, a miracle happened and a product called lipstain was birthed. The adverts went something like this: 'Soft and smooth, rich and nourishing, moisturising and conditioning formulation with vitamin E, which changes colour according to the pH of your skin. This long-lasting lip stain, which lasts over twelve hours, will stay put through kissing (air kissing, to be specific), eating (as long as it's only lettuce leaves eaten through a straw) and swimming (with a full-face mask), yet it will not stain a teacup (the quality of the porcelain having been dramatically improved).' Magic Lips came in a seductive range of colours, from creamy opaque to bright green, to create the perfect shade unique to you. The green stick turned my lips into a tangerine orange, whereas it rendered Lizzy's lips plum. Merely looking at the stick, you never knew what effect it was going to have on the colour of your mouth.

This was it! The perfect solution – a lip colour so resilient I would never need to reapply. It was guaranteed to survive a ten-hour flight, multiple cups of coffee and a greasy economy-class meal. Or so they said.

By the time I returned to the cockpit with the 'lip balm for chapped and dry lips', five tired-looking pilots and flight engineers stared back at me from the poorly lit capsule. Archie gratefully accepted the tube I offered him. In the dim light, he failed to spot the green colour and started applying it to his cracked lips with fervour. The other four chaps followed suit and then thanked me for sharing my lip salve with them. It was their gratitude that made me feel guilty. But only for a second.

We landed in Perth and the passengers started disembarking via the two forward doors on the left. The five cockpit crew had emerged from the flight deck, where they stood all broad-shouldered and butch in their smart uniforms, complete with caps, looking every inch like drag queens with their assortment of bright red, pink and orange lips as they nodded goodbye to the straggling passengers. If ever there was a successful advertisement for lip stain, this was it. Amen, ad agency! It might not always have worked as well for me, but it certainly did due diligence for the boys. Despite my best intentions, somebody is always bound to be offended. With great power comes great responsibility and it's no joke having the commander of the aircraft compete with the hosties on the make-up front. Poor

Archie was never right again after walking around Perth with red lips for two days.

Perth reminded me a lot of Cape Town, only without the trademark Table Mountain dominating the view, but the beaches were quite as beautiful and just as prolific. We visited Scarborough, with its chilled-out atmosphere. It was close to the shops and restaurants and stippled with loads of ice cream joints and cafés. Similarly, I loved all the activity that Cottesloe Beach offered, with its hordes of boogie boarders, runners and swimmers; it was like a picture postcard come to life.

But possibly my favourite place was the little port city, half an hour out of Perth, where the Swan River meets the Indian Ocean, called Fremantle. The winding streets of the pedestrian-friendly city still held the charm of a colonial background. It was vibrant and friendly, with buskers on every corner making music of one kind or another. People smiled. Everyone seemed happy and in love with life. It would've been exactly the right place to be on 26 September 1983, when the yacht *Australia II* made history. This was the day when the oldest sporting trophy in the world, the America's Cup, was wrested from the Americans after 132 years. It was still a good place to be on the same day, albeit one year later.

I'd never even heard of the America's Cup, but I was certainly being educated about it that day. The mood was contagious and Lizzy and I did not need much coaxing to join in the celebrations. We learnt that the America's Cup was a trophy awarded to the winner of a race between two yachts, the defender and the challenger. Any yacht club that met the requirements specified had the right to challenge the yacht club that held the cup, in an attempt to gain possession of it. There was an enormous amount of history and prestige associated with this coveted trophy, which attracted not only the world's top sailors and yacht designers, but also wealthy entrepreneurs and sponsors. *Australia II* was owned and built by a syndicate of Western Australians, headed by former businessman, Alan Bond. The syndicate had unsuccessfully challenged for the cup three times, which had been held by the New York Yacht Club since 1851. Australia was determined to bring home the 'auld mug' in 1983.

The yacht had been built in Cottesloe by local a boat builder. The crew, who had been based in Perth, had undertaken a rigorous training programme to prepare them for the series of races that would determine the challenger for the America's Cup, held in Newport, Rhode Island.

There had been a round robin series to select a challenger for the cup, and this yacht had then raced in the best of seven races to determine the ultimate winner. At the end of four races, the crew of *Australia II* was 3-1 down. They faced an enormous challenge. Against all the odds, *Australia II* went on to win the remaining three races, and so became the first non-American yacht to win the cup.

The whole country was celebrating the anniversary of this victory, but nowhere more so than in the little harbour town of Fremantle. What a privilege it was to celebrate with the locals.

It wasn't difficult to fill seventeen days in Perth. We could easily have visited a different beach each day and that would not even have made a dent in our two-and-a-half weeks' stay. But there were other things to do and experience.

Being good South Africans and loyal to our heritage, we felt compelled to undertake a wine cruise on the Swan River, in order to see how these wines compared to those of our world-renowned vineyards in the Cape. En route to buy our tickets, we bumped into Archie and invited him to come along. Without the stained lips, he was actually rather an attractive man. He had just left two of the other cockpit crew at the breakfast bar, fully intending to go for a run in an attempt to undo some of the damage inflicted by too many croissants. However, an invitation from a pair of hosties, especially when it involved alcohol, was a rare thing, not to be tossed aside. He suggested checking whether the other chaps might want to join us. He managed to enlist both – Pete, the co-pilot and Danny, the flight engineer.

We made our way to the ticket booth at Elizabeth Quay on the edge of the Swan River and eventually boarded the boat. It was touristy, but fun, as we cruised into the upper regions of the Swan Valley, leaving behind the iconic city skyline. Whenever even a handful of crew got together, you could be assured of noise and nonsense. Our men regaled anyone who would listen with their tale of woe at having been tricked into using lipstick. I tried to re-engineer the look to add to the authenticity of their story, but no amount of cajoling could get them to fall into the same trap again. The rest of the passengers gathered around our little group, as they were coerced into drinking beers at an ungodly hour of the morning. And they weren't even Aussies. I noticed Archie draping his arm around Lizzy's shoulders in a proprietary manner. She offered no resistance. When the boat docked at our first stop, we were having such a good time that we were reluctant to get off. And we'd made so many new friends! However, the promise of food was enough to make us move. Lizzy and I had not even had breakfast and the alcohol on our empty stomachs was beginning to take effect. We were treated to an outstanding lunch at the popular Sandalford Estate, where we had a behind-the-scenes tour of the vineyard, before getting to taste a multitude of fine wines.

The return journey was a lot noisier than the outbound one, as we stopped along the way to sample yet more Western Australian wines. This was accompanied by afternoon tea and cakes, in an attempt to soak up some of the alcohol. The music was turned up and dancing up and down the aisles of the boat was encouraged. By now, Lizzy was firmly ensconced in the crook of Archie's elbow so I ended up fraternising not only with our very own boys, but also the boat crew – I couldn't resist the gold braid on the epaulettes. Once a cockpit fly, always a cockpit fly.

By the time we got back to Perth, the sun was setting. We zig-zagged our way back to the hotel and ended up in Archie's room for the obligatory nightcap. By this stage, Lizzy and Archie had eyes only for each other, albeit that they were very blurry, bloodshot eyes. Lizzy had never displayed a great fondness for alcohol, but a full day of wine tasting could derail even the most ardent teetotaller. Pete, Danny and I discreetly departed. I would catch up with Lizzy in the morning and no doubt get a full rundown of the events of the night.

The following day, I was awoken by loud knocking on my door, even louder than the noise made by an invisible hammer, which was banging away at the inside of my head right behind my left eye. I let Lizzy in and switched on the miniature portable kettle we all travelled with. She was buzzing – simultaneously excited by the hint of a new romantic adventure and mortified by the fact that she could not quite remember the exact sequence of events the night before. She even confessed that she wasn't 100 per cent sure if they had in fact done the dirty deed. 'Get dressed, we're all meeting up for breakfast in half an hour,' she said after downing her coffee. 'Knock on my door when you're ready.'

We always requested inter-leading rooms if possible, and if not, rooms right next door to each other. So, a half an hour later, revived after a hot shower, I tapped on her door. She emerged, looking radiant, and we ambled down the road. Lizzy was still on a high and, I could tell, excited about meeting the chaps for breakfast – in particular one chap. Unfortunately, Archie had clearly had an epiphany during the early hours of the morning. Either that, or the excessive consumption of alcohol the night before had completely obliterated his memory. There was no display of affection for my friend. Even recognition was scant. There are times when sobriety can be a curse. To make matters worse, he actively started making a play for me! I winced at witnessing Lizzy's utter humiliation. It was as if the Brothers Grimm had rewritten the fairy tale and after the prince had kissed Sleeping Beauty he banished her back to the glass coffin just as she was about to wake up, stretch her arms above her head and enjoy the birdsong. No way were we going to let this heartless Casanova come between us. I looked around for a poisoned apple. There were never any around when you needed one. We threw a few dollars on the counter and took our leave, without as much as a backward glance.

Lizzy was spitting, 'Why do I always manage to attract horrible men who are sex maniacs with commitment issues and who drink too much?'

'Because the nice sex maniacs with commitment issues who drink too much are gay,' I told her.

We decided then and there that we would cope perfectly fine on our own, without male company for the remainder of our seventeen-day trip. We took ourselves off to Cottesloe Beach for the rest of the afternoon, where we lay in the sunshine, bodies oiled like the underbelly of peppered mackerel and slated the universal male population with ferocity, until we felt an inner peace descend upon us. In the evening we caught a bus back to the hotel, where we studiously avoided anyone who bore a vague resemblance to an SAA pilot. After a quick change of clothing, we zipped out and found a quaint little restaurant, where we perused a stash of brochures and hatched plans for the following day.

No trip to Perth would be complete without a visit to Rottnest Island. It was easy to arrange – just a quick ferry ride across the water. Dressed in shorts and trainers, with rucksacks on our backs, we arrived on the little island and went in search of bike hire. With no cars on the island, which was only 11km long and 4.5km wide, it seemed like the ideal choice of transportation.

Cycling around the circumference of the island, with its beautiful bays and coral reefs, was fantastic. Wherever I looked, I was surrounded by pristine water, varying in shades from pale blue to turquoise.

Rottnest has a rich history and is best known for its population of quokkas, a small native marsupial which in fact, gave rise to the name of this tiny island. It was the Dutch sailor, Willem de Vlamingh, who landed there in 1696 and mistook these animals for giant rats. He called it Rotte nest – rat's nest. After the British settlers arrived and established the Swan River Colony in 1829, the island has variously hosted a penal colony, military installations and interment camps. But since the 1900s the island has been largely devoted to recreational use.

We stopped in a bay with a rickety jetty and spread ourselves out on the sand. Our rucksacks were filled with water, snacks and a bottle of wine. It was idyllic – warm and windless. Before making myself too comfortable, I decided to go off in search of a loo.

That was harder than I thought and took a lot longer than I'd anticipated. By the time I made it back down the steps to where I had left Lizzy on the beach, she was nowhere to be seen. Two striped towels lay side by side, two discarded bicycles propped up next to them. At this point, most people would have felt those icy tentacles of fear snaking all around their bodies, but I knew better than to panic. I knew exactly where to find my friend. The beautiful yacht moored beside the jetty was a dead give-away.

I ambled closer. Seated on the back of the boat, nibbling from a plate of roast chicken and a variety of salads, with a crystal glass of what to me looked very much like chilled champagne in one hand, was Lizzy. Four gregarious sailors waved at me. All men. Funny that.

Lizzy and I had developed a code of communication a couple of months prior. It had been born out of necessity. Before 'the incident', we had successfully used a foreign language to convey undercover messages. We both spoke German, which came in handy when, at various times at different places in the world, we had felt an irresistible urge to discuss something as critical as the length of the nose hairs of the barman serving us a drink in New York, or the state of an unsuspecting bus conductor's teeth. We'd have a right old gossip about the poor sod under scrutiny, as he innocently carried on serving us, or simply continued to exist, totally oblivious to the flaws we had identified.

It generally worked well, except for the time we were travelling on a bus and could not help but notice the unusual-looking gentleman sitting on the opposite aisle seat. Lizzy felt compelled to state the obvious – just in case I had not clocked his porcine features. Intuitively knowing what she was about to do, I shook my head from side to side. I didn't want people to know that we were together. I squashed myself against the window, trying to put as much distance as I could between us. It was at this point that I felt like suggesting she could be East Germany and I'd be West. Ignoring my desperate attempts to silence her, she blundered ahead without bothering to keep her voice down – she was speaking in German after all, '*Er hat ein Gesicht wie ein Schwein.*' (He has a face like a pig). I was mortified on his behalf. The man turned to her, shoved his piggy face within millimetres of hers and said, '*Danke*' and then promptly got off the bus. It was then that she looked out of the window and saw the sign that said, '*Willkommen in Wiesbaden.*' No amount of linguistic acrobatics was going to get her out of that situation. That's what too much travel does – confuses the hell out of you. And she couldn't even blame it on jet lag.

We learnt our lesson from that little experience and thus a new non-verbal means of covert communication was established. It involved the removal of an item, such as a jacket or a pair of sunglasses, which meant 'no', or the use of it, which meant a definite 'yes'. The person asking the question would make an obvious overture of touching said item, so that the other one knew how to respond.

I was invited to step on board and a glass of bubbles was shoved into my hand. I introduced myself; they passed around Fosters. Bruce, Bruce, Bruce and Bruce seemed like nice enough guys. They were a lot older than we were – at least forty. I wondered if this was a good idea. We were in such a remote place that nobody would ever find us, should things turn nasty. In fact, no-one in the world even knew that, at that very moment, I was on Rottnest Island at all. I made a point of asking them about their wives and the domesticity of their lives. The response was as expected – they were all happily married and their wives had, in fact, packed their cooler boxes with all the gorgeous salads, chicken and beers. I couldn't help but wonder which wife had packed the champagne for a chance meeting with two young air hostesses.

The mood was light. The boat bobbed on the ocean. A breeze soft as a butterfly's wings blew through my hair, as we chatted easily with the four guys. As the sun began to make its way down in the west and an orange glow started to settle on the water, it was time to say goodbye and start our cycle ride back to the ferry point. I have to admit, I felt slightly relieved that we had survived the encounter and not been chopped up by meat cleavers, only to have our body parts discovered in various freezers scattered across Australia six months later. In fairness, they didn't seem the type though, but you never know. I'll bet Jack the Ripper was a right charmer when he wanted to be.

It was at this point, when we were about to make a dash to safety, that one of the chaps suggested they sail us back to the harbour in Perth. The other three concurred immediately. My heart sank – we were so close to escape from these possible axe murderers. Perhaps it was all part of their ploy? My mother had warned me about older men.

I looked at Lizzy. She plunged her hand into her handbag and pulled out a pair of Jackie O sunglasses, which she ceremoniously put onto her face. It was a 'YES' from her. Panic surged through my body. But only for one half of a second. The idea of cruising into Perth harbour in the sunset seemed infinitely preferable to a cycle ride, followed by a ferry ride, followed by a bus ride. I'd take my chances. I slipped my shades onto my face, 'Let's just get our bikes.' We would return them to the port in Perth the next day. So much for avoiding the company of men for the remainder of our stay in Australia.

That turned out to be one of the best decisions I've made. It rated right up there with the football match in London. The Perth skyline was magnificent, as the coloured lights from the lit-up buildings were reflected in the calm waters of the bay. Our sailors were competent as they manoeuvred the yacht into its slot, collected their belongings and waved us goodbye, without as much as a lewd comment, or a request to see us again. Bona fide gentlemen.

12

THE HELDERBERG DISASTER

It was the morning of 28 November 1987. I was awoken very early in the day to the news that South African Airways Flight 295 had disappeared off the radar screens. Even I knew that it was not possible to misplace an entire Jumbo Jet. It could mean only one thing ... the plane had gone down.

I had travelled down to Durban for the wedding of a longstanding family friend. His new bride was to become one of my very closest friends from that day onwards. My mom and I were staying in the delightful little seaside cottage of yet other longstanding family friends – totally unrelated, but so close that they may as well have been family. So much so that my brother and I called them Uncle and Aunty.

Listening to the news on the radio was like taking a cannonball in the stomach. Instinctively, I wanted to switch it off, remain in denial, but at the same time, in some macabre fashion, I was drawn to it. Like self-flagellation, I wanted more. The more I heard, the more it hurt. The hideous truth stared me perniciously in the face. Fear surged through my body and scorched my insides, like a rampant bush fire. Where were my friends? Who was on that plane? The overriding physical memory I have was one of nausea. My mom and I looked at each other without saying a word, but I saw the guilt in her eyes. She was thanking God for not letting me be on that plane. That's all that mattered to her. She knew better than to voice that opinion.

From somewhere in the little holiday house, the phone rang. I heard Uncle Viv answer it and then his footsteps on the tiles, as he padded towards our room. 'It's Jasper,' he said through the closed door. My dad.

As I came out of the room, my mom hot on my heels, Uncle Viv hugged me. He, too, had heard the news. Nestled in the arms of this huge, compassionate man, I felt safe. I even allowed myself to briefly wonder if my world had really collapsed, or if I had just imagined it.

He pointed to the phone and I picked up the handset, dangling on a cord from the base which was mounted on the wall. How reassuring it was to hear my father's voice on the other end of the line. But, despite that, all I could do was cry. I handed the instrument to my mom.

Daddy was so relieved to hear our voices. Apparently he had been inundated with calls from many of their friends, on hearing about the disaster. They all knew that I was an air hostess with the national carrier and felt compelled to check that I was alright. It seemed that eventually, after so many calls, even my father began to doubt himself. He knew that we had flown to Durban for the wedding but, at the same time, he also knew just how fond I was of the Mauritius/Hong Kong/Taipei route. He needed to hear my voice to make sure he hadn't lost his mind, or somehow got it wrong, and that I was safe.

We gathered in the lounge – a motley little crew of four, in our dressing-gowns. With dour faces and stooped shoulders, we glanced at the waves crashing upon the rocks in front of us – a scene at which we would normally marvel. But now the serenity of it was lost in the inner turmoil, as the television screen in the corner of the room fought for our attention. We were in a state of disbelief; these things just didn't happen so close to home. Snippets of news kept coming through.

The Boeing 747-244B Combi had taken off from Taipei's Chiang Kai Shek International Airport the afternoon before, en route to Johannesburg, via Mauritius. Dawie Uys was the captain of the flight. I knew him, but not well.

I was grateful to be in a warm, home environment with such caring people, instead of in a cold, austere hotel room. Aunty Olga fussed around, bringing endless mugs of coffee and rusks through from the kitchen. With her strong Mauritian-French accent, she frequently lightened the sombre atmosphere with her unique expressions and misuse of the English language. 'You think maybe it was an eye-jack?'

The Helderberg was 7 years old and one of the two Combi aircraft in SAA's fleet. These aeroplanes carried both passengers and air freight on the main deck, although in different compartments. There was a small door at the rear of the passenger cabin allowing entry into the cargo section. There was netting just inside the door, presumably to prevent the shifting of cargo in-flight. I once had been on a flight with Aldo Cloutard, on this very aircraft. He was one of the most entertaining stewards you could ever wish to fly with, who always maintained a deadpan face while uttering the most outrageous statements which most passengers fell for hook, line and sinker. On that particular flight, Aldo waltzed down the aisle with me trying to keep up behind him in puppy dog fashion, broadcasting for the benefit of all and sundry, 'Come and help me, Doll. We've got to feed the elephants.' The passengers at the rear of the plane twisted their necks, eyes the size of cricket balls, as he opened the door and whooshed into the tail end of the plane. His voice rang out from the cavernous hollow, 'OK, boys, here's your straw. Dumbo! Get your trunk away from me!' I was left standing at the door, grinning like an idiot, unable to be his accomplice in this deceit, despite my best efforts.

He came out of the cargo compartment, wrist held to his forehead as he banged the door closed. With the swagger of a current-day footballer, he then strode back down the aisle, opening and closing the overhead stowages with as much theatrics as he could muster, asking, 'Are all the babies in the hat racks?' It was impossible to keep a straight face when Aldo Cloutard was on board. Once, on a flight with him, after a particularly long and tiring service, we finally reached the stage of offering our passengers tea and coffee. By this stage, we could all do with a little light entertainment. Aldo parked the trolley and leaned over towards a passenger, cup on a small tray in his left hand and big metal pot in his right. 'Tea or coffee,' he asked.

'Coffee,' answered the man.

'Wrong! It's tea,' said Aldo and pushed the trolley forward to serve the next row of people. The passengers loved him. The crew bid to be on his flights.

The news continued its drip-feed of information. I was riveted. Apparently, the crew had reported smoke aboard the aircraft about nine hours after take-off. They had been in communication with the control tower at Plaisance Airport in Mauritius. Nothing more at this stage.

Reluctantly my mom and I pulled ourselves away from the TV and got dressed for the wedding. I felt discombobulated, not really in the present. It was as if a fog had swept into my head and remained there, teasing me and twirling around my brain. I felt a desperation to know who was on that flight. I knew that Lizzy wasn't on it, thank God, as she was going to pop by the wedding reception later to say hello. She, too, was visiting her parents, who lived close to Durban. Besides which, Lizzy and I were practically conjoined twins when it came to flying to the Far East; it was unlikely that she'd have done that route without me. More than the Orient, we especially enjoyed the Mauritius layover on that routing. We would have two days and a night on either side of the Johannesburg leg, i.e. en route to Hong Kong, as well as on the return from Taipei. In Mauritius, we usually got up early in the mornings, before the heat kicked in, and played hours of tennis and squash. We had become friendly with the local coaches of both these sports, who themselves were only too pleased to have a competitive game with us. They welcomed the break from the humdrum coaching of novices on holiday trying out a new sport.

These were the days before mobile phones. Hard to imagine how we survived without them. In today's world of instant communication, it would've been so much easier to locate everyone I cared about. Facebook would have been invaluable at a time like this. There was nothing to do but to sit it out.

It's an amazing thing to witness how a disaster of such sensational magnitude unites people. When we arrived at the church, it was clear that everyone was distraught by this tragic event. Words like, 'I just can't believe it!' 'What do you think could have happened?' spilled off people's lips. Folks looked to me as a wise oracle on a missing Jumbo Jet. Being a 'trolley dolly' gave me no more insight into the mystery of the missing plane than the priest in his purple robes performing the nuptials. If anybody should have had a hotline, he would've been in the queue before me. But he knew as little as I did.

I made a concerted effort not to let this devastating event detract from the bride's special day and similarly, the guests put on their party faces and all sombre decorum was quashed. I looked at the positive side – it was good to have a happy event to focus on.

Throughout the wedding reception, which was held in a splendid marquee in the garden of the family home, I kept nipping off to the lounge to gather the latest news.

The plane had been officially declared missing, with 140 passengers and nineteen crew. As the names of the flight deck crew were being made public, I sat, frozen with apprehension. Please God, let it not be anybody I knew well. I knew that wasn't a fair request; I felt selfish and heartless, but it was so much easier when people who perished in a disaster were only names to you. After the captain, the next name to be released was that of First Officer, David Atwell. A jolt shook my body as the pleasant, open face appeared on the TV screen. I vividly recalled a recent trip to Spain with Dave and his fiancée, Magda, who was also an air hostess. A crowd of us had travelled to a town called Sanguesa, where we put bravery before sense and ran with the bulls, a precursor to Pamplona. Now they were both gone. It felt surreal. But it was the appearance on the screen of the next name that completely undid me. The relief co-pilot on that flight was Geoffrey Birchall. That couldn't be! Not a man of such unerring optimism and sense of fun. I couldn't help thinking that if I felt so completely hollow, how would his family and close friends be feeling? My heart broke for them. Images of the flights I had done with Geoff ran through my mind – everyone involved laughing, until my sides felt as though they would tear apart. His penchant for humour and mischief would be sorely missed by every single person who'd had the privilege of knowing him. I was always delighted to see Geoff's name on the crew list, or spot him in the right-hand seat of the cockpit when I went to introduce myself, as it meant that not only would I have somebody to play tennis with but, more importantly, the guarantee of a good giggle.

As more names appeared on the screen, it became obvious that, at some stage or another, I had flown with every single one of those crew members who lost their lives that day. It could just as easily have been me.

In the weeks and months that followed, it was ascertained that at some point during the flight, a fire had developed in the cargo section of the main deck. In what became one of the deepest successful salvage operations ever conducted, one of the flight data recorders was recovered from a depth of around 4,900m. This would be the start of an official enquiry into the cause of the fire, leading to a number of conspiracy theories over the years.

Aircraft are fitted with a cockpit voice recorder (CVR) to record sounds in the cockpit which, in the event of an accident, could assist in an investigation. The tape capacity is limited, so on this particular flight, at any given time, only the last thirty minutes would be available for playback. Unfortunately, in this instance, due to damage from the massive fire, the tape did not cover the estimated twenty minutes of the flight prior to impact.

It is impossible to imagine the fear in that cabin and yet the professional calm amongst the cockpit crew was remarkable. They were well aware of the emergency situation with which they were dealing, yet by the sounds of it, they maintained level-headed and unruffled communication throughout. It was captured in the spine-chilling transcript of the eighty-second CVR recording*, as well as the recorded conversation between Flight 295 and MRU, which appeared in the Report of the Board of Inquiry into the Helderberg Air Disaster.

Time (sec)	CVR Recording
0	Fire alarm bell (stopped very quickly by the crew).
4	Intercom chime.
5	Flight engineer: 'What's going on now?'
6	Unknown: 'Huh?'
9	Flight engineer: 'Cargo?'
11	Flight engineer: 'It came on now afterwards'
14	Strong click sound.
14	Unknown: 'And where is that?'
15	Click sound.
17	Possibly flight engineer: 'Just to the right'
18	Unknown: 'Say again (?)'
21	Flight engineer: 'Main deck cargo'
26	Flight engineer: 'Than the other one came on as well, I've got two'
30	Flight engineer: 'Shall I (get/push) the (bottle/button) over there'
31	Unknown: 'Ja (yes)'
34	Captain: 'Read the check list there for us please'

---

* www.lessonslearned.faa.gov/SA295/Transcript_CVR_MRU.pdf (accessed 22 July 2016).

34	Double click sound.
37	Unknown: 'The breaker fell out as well'
38	Unknown: 'Huh'
38	(Two click sounds).
41	Captain: 'Yes'
41	Sounds of movement can be heard with clicks and clunks.
62	Captain: '___ it is the fact that both came on – it disturbs me'
65	Intercom chime (while captain is speaking).
67	Unknown: 'Aag ___'
69	800 Hz TEST TONE signal commences.
70	Captain: 'What the ___ is going on now?'
73	Sudden loud sound.
75	Large and rapid changes in amplitude of test tone start.
80	End of test signal, very irregular near end.
81	End of recording.

Several minutes likely elapsed after the CVR malfunctioned, before the conversation with MRU (Mauritius) commenced. It is likely that during this time, the flight crew continued to carry out their procedures associated with fire and smoke.

Following is a transcript of the communications between Flight 295 and MRU that were recorded by MRU. At some points in the recording, communications between cockpit crewmembers can be heard. Times identified below represent local time in Mauritius. Transmissions are in English, except as noted.

Time	Who	Recording
23:48:51	Flight 295	'Eh, Mauritius, Mauritius, Springbok Two Niner Five'
23:49:00	MRU	'Springbok Two Niner Five, eh, Mauritius, eh, good morning, eh, go ahead'
23:49:07	Flight 295	'Eh, good morning, we have, eh, a smoke, eh, eh, problem and we're doing emergency descent to level one five, eh, one four zero'
23:49:18	MRU	'Confirm you wish to descend to flight level one four zero'
23:49:20	Flight 295	'Ya, we have already commenced, eh, due to a smoke problem in the aeroplane'
23:49:25	MRU	'Eh, roger, you are clear to descend immediately to flight level one four zero'
23:49:30	Flight 295	'Roger, we will appreciate if you can alert, eh, fire, eh, eh, eh, eh'
23:49:40	MRU	'Do you wish to, eh, do you request a full emergency?'
23:49:48	Flight 295	'(Okay Joe, can you … for us),' spoken in Afrikaans.
23:49:51	MRU	'Springbok Two Nine Five, Plaisance.'
23:49:54	Flight 295	'Sorry, go ahead'

Time	Who	Recording
23:49:56	MRU	'Do you, eh, request a full emergency please a full emergency?'
23:50:00	Flight 295	'Affirmative, that's Charlie Charlie'
23:50:02	MRU	'Roger, I declare a full emergency, roger'
23:50:04	Flight 295	'Thank you'
23:50:40	MRU	'Springbok Two Nine Five, Plaisance.'
23:50:44	Flight 295	'Eh, go ahead'
23:50:46	MRU	'Request your actual position please and your DME Distance'
23:50:51	Flight 295	'Eh, we haven't got the DME yet'
23:50:55	MRU	'Eh, roger and your actual position please'
23:51:00	Flight 295	'Eh, say again'
23:51:02	MRU	'Your actual position'
23:51:08	Flight 295	'Now we've lost a lot of electrics, we haven't got anything on the aircraft now'
23:51:12	MRU	'Eh roger, I declare a full emergency immediately'
23:51:15	Flight 295	'Affirmative'
23:51:18	MRU	'Roger'
23:52:19	MRU	'Eh, Springbok Two Nine Five, do you have an Echo Tango Alfa Plaisance please'

Time	Who	Recording
23:52:30	MRU	'Springbok Two Nine Five, Plaisance'
23:52:32	Flight 295	'Ya, Plaisance'
23:52:33	MRU	'Do you have an Echo Tango Alfa Plaisance please'
23:52:36	Flight 295	'Ya, eh, zero zero, eh eh eh three zero.'
23:52:40	MRU	'Roger, zero zero three zero, thank you'
23:52:50	Flight 295	'Hey Joe, shut down the oxygen left'
23:52:52	MRU	'Sorry say again please'
00:01:34	Flight 295	'Eh Plaisance, Springbok Two Nine Five, we've opened the door(s) to see if we (can?)…we should be okay'
00:01:36	Flight 295	'Look there (?)' (Exclamation by somebody else, and is said over the last part of the previous sentence)
00:01:45	Flight 295	'(Close the bloody door)' spoken in Afrikaans.
00:01:57	Flight 295	'Joe, switch up quickly, then close the hole on your side'
00:02:10	Flight 295	'Pressure (?) Twelve thousand'
00:02:14	Flight 295	'(is enough … otherwise our flight could come to grief!)' Spoken in Afrikaans.

Time	Who	Recording
00:02:25	Flight 295	Carrier wave only
00:02:38	Flight 295	'Eh Plaisance, Springbok Two Nine Five, do (did) you copy'
00:02:41	MRU	'Eh negative, Two Nine Five, say again please, say again'
00:02:43	Flight 295	'We're now sixty five miles'
00:02:45	MRU	'Confirm sixty five miles'
00:02:47	Flight 295	'Ya, affirmative Charlie Charlie'
00:02:50	MRU	'Eh, Roger, Springbok eh Two Nine Five, eh, re you're recleared flight level five zero. Recleared flight level five zero'
00:02:58	Flight 295	'Roger, five zero'
00:03:00	MRU	'And, Springbok Two Nine Five copy actual weather Plaisance. The wind one one zero degrees zero five knots. The visibility above one zero kilometres. And we have a precipitation in sight to the north. Clouds, five octas one six zero zero, one octa five thousand feet. Temperature twenty two, two, two. And the QNH one zero one eight hectopascals, one zero one eight over.'
00:03:28	Flight 295	'Roger, one zero one eight'
00:03:31	MRU	'Affirmative, eh and both runways available if you wish'

Time	Who	Recording
00:03:43	MRU	'And two nine five, I request pilot's intention'
00:03:46	Flight 295	'Eh, we'd like to track in eh, on eh one three'
00:03:51	MRU	'Confirm runway one four'
00:03:54	Flight 295	'Charlie Charlie'
00:03:56	MRU	'Affirmative and you're cleared, eh direct to Foxtrot Foxtrot. You report approaching five zero'
00:04:02	Flight 295:	'Kay'
00:08:00	MRU:	'Two Nine Five, Plaisance'
00:08:11	MRU:	'Springbok Two Nine Five, Plaisance'
00:08:35	MRU:	'Springbok Two Nine Five, Plaisance'
END*		

An official board of enquiry was established to determine the cause of and culpability for the accident. This search and recovery process took two years. The wreckage had to be located and then recovered. At a depth of 45km, this sea salvage remains the deepest-ever successful recovery operation to date. Of the two vital items that provide clues in any accident investigation, only the Cockpit Voice Recorder (CVR) was retrieved. The Digital Flight Data Recorder (DFDR) was never found.

* www.lessonslearned.faa.gov/SA295/Transcript_CVR_MRU.pdf (accessed 22 July 2016)

The Board of Enquiry found that the firefighting and safety equipment on this type of aircraft were outdated and woefully inadequate, which immediately led to SAA discontinuing the use of Combi aircraft. What they were unable to establish, however, is what caused the massive fire and how exactly the aircraft came to crash into the sea.

This led to a number of conspiracy theories, which to this day still abound. The most popular belief is that the South African government (under an arms embargo at the time) had to buy arms clandestinely and had therefore placed a rocket system in the cargo hold. The vibrations led to the unstable rocket fuel igniting. Another theory is that the South African Defence Force was smuggling red mercury on the flight for its atomic bomb project. Yet another theory alleges that activated carbon had been placed on board. While that dependable old sinner – the apartheid government – may well have been responsible for many disasters, it is unlikely that they would have ordered a salvage operation at this exorbitant cost if it could have implicated them. Surely, in light of this almost impossible operation, they would have rather gleefully rubbed their hands, knowing that their dirty secret could never be uncovered, and simply said, 'Sorry about the crash guys; too deep to find the wreckage' and left it at that. Instead, they threw millions of rands at the project named 'Operation Resolve' in order to uncover the facts.

The most outrageous theory alleges that there were two fires on board. Apparently, the first fire was extinguished but then – so the story goes – the captain of the plane was 'ordered' to continue on to Johannesburg, instead of doing what any well-trained pilot would have done, which was divert to the nearest alternate airport. Conspiracy theories are generally irrational and this is no exception because, in the first instance, no captain would take this decision on his own. The entire cockpit crew – consisting of three pilots and two flight engineers – would need to agree to not only this illegal arrangement, but also agree to remain silent in the face of interrogation by the powers that be. This bizarre proposition is tantamount to flying an aeroplane in a compromised situation, whereby the captain would say, 'Sorry, guys, we've lost three engines and both wings, but we need to carry on. Apparently, the South African Defence Force has told the Minister of Defence to tell the head of airline to tell us that we have to plough on.' Laughable.

Recently, a newer theory has been presented by the South African investigative journalist, Mark Young, who suggests that a short circuit in the on-board electronics may have caused the fire. This so-called 'wet arc tracking' was similarly responsible for the Swiss Air crash in 1998.

Whatever caused the massive fire on board the Helderberg will, in all probability, never be known and undoubtedly the conspiracy theories will continue.

For many months after the catastrophe, the subject was on everybody's minds. Each crew I flew with intermittently speculated on the cause of the accident and recalled humorous incidents with our fellow crew members who had perished. But strangely, it did not galvanise a single one of us to contemplate resigning from the airline.

At dinner parties, my non-airline friends were riveted by this disaster and clamoured for inside information. Everybody had become an authority on the Helderberg. This prompted them to talk about various flights they'd been on – flights from hell, where they were convinced they were going to die. But the reality was, air travel was safe, much safer than driving a car and especially true in my case. In fact, I could quite confidently say that if you put twenty air crew with gazillions of years of flying hours between them, in the same room, you'd be hard-pressed to hear a single story of a life-threatening flight they'd been on. In contrast, some flights could be touch and go for passengers due to overreactions of crew in response to a persistent call bell, but they were a rarity and the victims generally survived.

The only in-flight emergency I was ever involved in turned out not to be an emergency at all. Just my luck – nothing to boast about, regaling people with stories about how I kept everyone calm and helped them down emergency chutes, with not a thought in the world for my own safety. In fact, I was barely aware that we were in the midst of an emergency situation. As we were gathering speed up the runway in preparation for lift-off, there was a major thump. I didn't really take much notice, because it felt quite similar to the time when I'd reversed over my ex-fiancé's golf clubs. My car was absolutely fine. Clearly, it was more serious when driving over something in a 747 on a runway. The pilots suspected that we'd lost a nose wheel, but we were too far gone to abort the take-off. They informed the cabin crew of the situation by means of a 5-5 call (emergency call from cockpit to all stations) and radioed the control tower. Air Traffic Control advised that nothing was visible on the runway. We were requested to do a fly-around as close as possible to the tower, in order for them to visually ascertain if we were in possession or not of said nose wheel. This would've been fine in a little aerobatic bi-plane, but it's not easy stuffing 279 people into one of those and charging exorbitant prices, so we attempted the fly-by in the jumbo. We never got close. Even with the aid of the Hubble telescope, it would've been impossible to spot a killer whale dangling from the undercarriage of a plane from that distance.

So, we continued on the flight to Cape Town. A landing-gear issue was not deemed to be a life-or-death situation. Of course not – as long as you were on another plane. That's what the captain told us anyway. I liked his confidence. We were briefed to prepare for an emergency landing and possibly an evacuation as well. The passengers were shown how to assume the brace position, while at the same time being told that all would be well on landing, it was simply a precautionary measure. Like wearing a bulletproof vest before a firing squad.

As we approached DF Malan airport in Cape Town, the runway was crawling with fire engines and emergency vehicles, lights flashing. In preparation for a belly landing, the landing strip had been sprayed with foam, preparing us for as soft an impact as possible under the circumstances. As we came closer and closer to touch down, the cabin was eerily silent. Nobody knew what to expect. It was probably the gentlest landing I'd ever experienced. Turned out the nose wheel had been there all along. Must have been the golf clubs again.

South Africans, as a nation, have a trait that is peculiar to us and that is the manner in which we use humour to deal with a disaster. This aircraft accident was no exception. There is always the risk of offending, especially people who are directly affected by the trauma, and yet, the minute disaster strikes, the jokes start flying (if you'll excuse the pun). It is not in any way a sign of disrespect; it is simply the tool this nation uses to pick themselves up, dust themselves off and start all over again. The first joke started the rounds within hours of the air crash, 'Who were the only people who benefited from the Helderberg?' The answer: 'The 'Fly Now, Pay Later' passengers.'

13

MERRIMENT IN MAINZ

At some stage during my airline career, SAA decided that they were going to place a security official on every single flight out of South Africa. I do not recall what the threat was, but so it came to pass that a new game was birthed amongst the cabin crew. It was called: 'Spot Matlock'. It was impossible to lose.

Generally, people dressed well in preparation for a flight in those earlier days. Apart from the few first-time fliers in economy class, who thought it fitting to bring along a set of pyjamas for the overnight trip. You gotta love them – they had no idea what to expect. They had this vision of a general hospital ward, where a curtain was whizzed around each individual to ensure their privacy and guarantee a good night's sleep. Their disappointment was heart-breaking. To them, not to us. Especially when they thought that coughing up the huge cost of an economy-class air ticket, on an international flight, had actually bought them pretty much the entire plane.

While tracksuits were the favoured attire on outbound flights in economy class, there was a much more sophisticated – though not prescribed – dress code in first and business classes. Or as we called them, 'the haves and the have yachts'. So revered were these sections of a plane that children under sixteen were not permitted to be seated in these areas, irrespective of how much money their parents were prepared to throw at it. There was absolutely no flexibility in this regard. The rule was set in place for the benefit of the privileged passengers who had forked out the full fare for the luxury and comfort of this mode of travel. Kids were barely allowed to slow down as they passed through this holy ground, en route to cattle class.

The nouveau riche had to make decisions. Or not. They were easy to spot in their designer jeans and T-shirts. Wealth had crept under their skins like poison, invading their posture and their gestures, as they waved their howling infants to the bowels of economy class with the nanny.

We had completed our preps for the flight to Frankfurt, when the economy class passengers started boarding. They filed in and shuffled down the two aisles to the tail end of the plane, as if they had crampons on their feet and were taking an arduous journey up the face of a snow-covered mountain. These were the ones who knew better than to expect the little privacy curtains. They were clearly in no rush to squeeze their 6ft 2in South African frames into 6.2in seats.

First- and business-class passengers always boarded at the end, having enjoyed the hospitality of the Blue Diamond courtesy lounge up until the very last minute. I was working in business class on this flight and welcomed our worthy passengers by name, as I had been trained to do. It was easier than it sounds – we had a list in the galley and put little stickers on the trolleys to help identify them according to their seat numbers. First-class passengers were whipped off to the left as they stepped onto the plane by the snooty senior bag, who did not want them to be contaminated by such low-life as myself. I was clearly only good enough up to a certain level.

Shirley (more about her later) and I greeted and seated our elegantly clad guests. Our eyes fell upon the male passenger in Row 7A, window seat. She and I looked at each other, winked and nodded our heads. Matlock. As easy as that. It was the cheap suit, the white shoes which my father would have referred to as 'brothel creepers', the broad, white, matching tie, black shirt and the comb in the pocket that did it. It was also the very broad Afrikaans accent that gave him away. These security guards were supposed to travel incognito, in order to foil a hijacking or terror attack of sorts and yet, they were always surprised when we identified them within seconds of them boarding. Impossible not to – they were all clones of one another. I wondered if there was a chance that they were actually issued with the outfits. Apparently not. None of us was ever entirely sure what their role as a free business-class passenger was, other than to educate themselves on the finer culinary aspects of life. All this flamboyant travel had certainly not done anything for their dress sense.

After the dinner service, once the lights had been switched off and most of the passengers were stretched out in the comfort of their business-class seats with their feet up, Shirley approached Matlock. The poor man was not allowed to shut his eyes for a single second. He had to remain vigilant, in case somebody tried to steal his shoes. But really, his duty was to protect us from some unseen threat. I wondered if this was where his comb was going to come in handy. That seemed the only reasonable explanation any man would walk around publicly with a comb sticking out of his pocket.

I heard her offering him a cup of coffee and then she asked as diplomatically as she could, 'Why don't you guys just dress a little better, blend in with the other passengers?' Her insult was totally lost on him as he answered, 'No, man, then we'll be too con-spishus!' That's been our catch-phrase ever since.

There had once been a successful hijacking of a SAA plane. It had happened in 1972. Perhaps that's why the management saw fit to employ the Matlock brigade in 1986. The reason it took fourteen years to implement was because it took that much time to gather together an equally badly dressed group of men, with combs in their pockets. The flight was en route from Salisbury in Rhodesia (now known as Harare in Zimbabwe) to Johannesburg. Two men, armed with a pistol, had placed dynamite sticks on the hat racks as they took control of the plane. The crew was forced to return to Salisbury, where they landed and refuelled. Twelve hostages were kept on board. The captain tricked them into believing that they were headed to the Seychelles. Instead, he made for Blantyre in Malawi. It was dark when they landed, which the passengers used to their advantage as they were moved into the cockpit by the flight steward and climbed down the emergency escape rope, without being seen. By the time the hijackers realised what had happened, only the captain, a flight steward and one passenger were still on board. The two hijackers then started fighting with each other, as they both wanted control of the dynamite fuse. This chaos allowed the final three captives to escape unnoticed. Once the hostages had made their break for freedom, the Malawian security forces started shooting at the plane until the hijackers surrendered. It was comforting to know that a repetition of this event was unlikely, due to the presence of our well-dressed, 'inconspishus' on-board security guards.

There was another security incident in January 1991. Up until the late '80s, South West Africa was under South African rule in a complex territorial mandate, finally gaining total independence in 1990 from whence it was known as Namibia. Similarly, the national carrier was originally known as Namib Air; after independence, this also changed to Air Namibia. Be that as it may, Air Namibia leased a Boeing SP aircraft from South African Airways. It was known as a wet lease, which meant that not only did they get the plane but they got the entire crew as well. No way were the bosses going to trust a newly independent airline with about $50 million worth of metal tube. Crew were expendable, planes weren't. Twenty cabin crew were selected to fly for Air Namibia. We wore our same navy blue SAA uniforms, but accessorised with a different scarf, as well as a differently shaped wing. We were also supplied with an Air Namibia 'crew card'.

A plane, duly painted in Air Namibia colours and thus flying under the auspices of that country, albeit manned by SAA crew, was sent from Johannesburg to Frankfurt via Windhoek. It was meant to have been empty on the outbound route, the intention being to bring back children – juvenile exiles who were sent to Germany from the then South West Africa, for their own safety until liberation. However, the marketing team was quick to spot an opportunity of increasing revenue and decided to load around forty passengers, who had been bumped off the SAA direct flight to Frankfurt. Naughty!

In the very early hours of the morning, the crew members were woken from slumber and told to hide their passports. The reason became clear when they noticed Russian MiG fighters on either side of the plane. The plane was forced to land in Algeria. Upon landing, military people with AK-47 assault rifles boarded the plane and tried to force the crew to disembark. For seven hours the captain remained calm and sensible as he negotiated his way out of the dilemma, explaining that the flight was from Windhoek and had absolutely nothing to do with the Gulf War, the invasion of Kuwait or, indeed, Saddam Hussein himself. Eventually, with the help of two German-speaking crew, he managed to convince the military men. Despite the unscheduled layover, which put all the crew well over their legal flight and duty time, the plane took off before you could say 'Fasten your seatbelts'. Never before and probably never again was anyone as pleased to land in Frankfurt, where the frosty welcome felt as warm as the embers of Hades. Once again, our newly appointed on-board security guards were conspicuous by their absence. Thank God for small mercies, as I fear they might have interpreted this disaster as an opportunity for spiritual and emotional growth that could have resulted in the entire crew and forty passengers ending their days in the Sahara Desert.

The rest of our flight to Frankfurt proceeded without incident. Some flights were like that. Unfortunately, not enough of them. I even managed to get a few hours of sleep in the crew rest and so arrived in this enormous city feeling fairly fresh – but that's a relative term. It simply meant that, for once, I didn't feel as though I had just emerged from the foggy haze of a general anaesthetic. That's as good as it gets. We boarded the bus for the half-hour journey to Mainz.

There can be very few small cities in the world quainter than Mainz. The university town lies right on the west bank of a romantic stretch of the Rhine, not far from where the mystical

Lorelei mermaid continues to enchant visitors. According to the legend, there once was a woman whose beauty caused sailors to wreck their ships, as they sailed along the river's edge, braving dangerous currents. This lore has a variety of versions, suggesting that it was her long, blonde hair that distracted sailors, as she lay sunbathing on the banks of the river, or perhaps she bewitched them with her clear voice and lured them with song.

The Mainz Hilton was perched right on the river, with scenic views and a constant gentle drift of boats going by. The hotel was stylish; it reeked of elegance and German efficiency. We stood in line beside the tall pine tree, which filled the foyer. It was covered in twinkling lights and a multitude of red, velvet bows. A fresh, mossy scent filled the air around it. Understated and elegant, this Christmas tree was testimony to the classy manner in which the Teutons displayed the onset of the festive season.

Clutching my keys, an envelope full of German Marks and my suitcase, I headed for the lift in search of my room. I dumped my bags, fished out my miniature of juniper juice and can of tonic and headed to Andy's room – he was the captain – for the debrief. For once I wasn't tired, but most of the others looked as though they had overdosed on sleeping tablets. The listless little gathering didn't last long. As they were filing out of the door, I noticed Andy's credit card–style room key on the bedside table and a demonic little voice in my ear told me to pick it up. A room key could always come in handy. At that stage, I had no idea in what manner it was going to be useful, but I pocketed it and said my goodbyes. I was sure we could hatch a plan.

I snuggled into my delicious German *Federbett* and had a few hours of blissful oblivion, despite the fact that I had not been very tired. You simply couldn't compete with a *Federbett* and win. It knocked the six out of any narcotic. An instant cure for insomnia.

When I woke up, I took myself off for a run along the banks of the river before meeting up with the rest of the gang in the late afternoon, for the short walk to the market square with the famed Dom Cathedral.

Generally, Mainz is captivating due to the open, friendly atmosphere of the town and its people, the twisting narrow lanes, the quaint shops and boutiques and gothic, timber-framed houses. It is filled with baroque buildings and imposing cathedrals. The *Altstadt* is the lively old quarter, where *Gemutlichkeit* flows out of every little pub with enchanting names like Doctor Flotte and fascinating streets called Heringsbrunnengasse and Augustinerstrasse. It is the world of sugar-candy cottages.

But Mainz at Christmas-time was in a different league. Against the backdrop of the 1,000-year-old cathedral, it was transformed into a fantasy. The historic market square had turned into a spectacle of lights, with strands strung from the high tower in the centre of the plaza to spots around the perimeter, like a glittering canopy. The air was filled with the spicy aroma of gingerbread and mulled wine. I pulled my coat tighter around me and inhaled the scent of cinnamon. Barrels of hot chestnuts and salty pretzels added a nutty, sweet smell, like a dry baked potato. Vendors, in decorated stalls resembling miniature chalets, sold advent garlands, straw stars and hearts, Christmas tree decorations, wooden toys, candles and other original, handmade crafts. Children with eager faces, lined up at the carousels. It felt for all the world as if I was wandering around in a Hans Christian Andersen bedtime story.

We gathered around a small wooden barrel, with a fire in the centre of it, as we sipped our *Gluhwein*. These glowing heaters were dotted all around the square, providing light and warmth to Christmas revellers.

Rolf's Pub was our next stop. It wasn't called Rolf's Pub at all and I don't think anyone in the airline ever knew its proper name. It was another typical idiosyncratically named venue, simply because the owner was called Rolf and for many years the crew had gone there, to the extent that Rolf and his family ended up visiting South Africa on many of their holidays.

I'd done a couple of Frankfurt flights and therefore been to Mainz a few times already, but somehow I'd never been introduced to this little gem before. I'd obviously hung out with the wrong crowd on my previous trips.

The small tavern was cosy, with wooden walls displaying the taxidermied heads of a variety of deer. These once-proud animals stared back at me with glazed eyes. Heavy-framed tapestries of gothic scenes were interspersed amongst the animal trophies. We sat at a round table, with a unique fireplace in the centre, over which hung a cylindrical, copper dome.

There was a feature of Rolf's pub that was iconic. It was a snuff machine. And it was legendary in the initiation of every airline member on their first visit to this bar. In this case, me. Despite my protests, vehement even by German standards, a wooden contraption was placed on the table in front of me and I was ordered to put my chin on the narrow wooden slab, which meant that my nose was resting on a thin timber bar. Before I was properly settled in, somebody hit the other end of the gadget with a heavy wooden mallet, thereby releasing a lethal dose of snuff, which went flying straight up my nasal cavities and blew my unsuspecting brain out of my ears. The impact was like being struck on the back of my head by a church bell. My eyes watered from the assault and my throat felt raw, as the mucus from my nose dripped down in protest.

There is a term in German – *Schadenfreude* – which means the satisfaction or pleasure felt at someone else's misfortune. My workmates were overdosing on it, clearly grateful that it was me and not them who had been at the receiving end of the snuff machine.

As the hit of nicotine dissipated, I started plotting revenge. I had Andy's room key in my possession, after all. Over our *Schweinehaxe*, *Eisbein* and *Sauerkraut*, we made our plans, oblivious to our captain. Each time he disappeared off to the gents or turned his head for a second, we collaborated in furious whispers. Shirley would have the star role. As a drama major at uni, this little act would be pips.

Shortly after dinner, five of us begged fatigue and departed, leaving Shirley behind with Andy – ever the gentleman – to keep her company, as she prolonged finishing off the last few drops of wine in her goblet. They would not be far behind us. I felt a bit guilty – Andy was such a lovely, gentle soul. And he wasn't even the one who'd delivered the toxic blow to the snuff machine, leading to my near-death experience. But, there was nothing to be done about it – his was the room key I held and thus an opportunity not to be squandered. It didn't usually come about as easily as this.

We hurried back to the hotel, without pausing to admire the sights and sounds of the Christmas market this time, and headed straight to Andy's room. The childishness of it all made us erupt into fits of giggles as we hid ourselves in cupboards and behind doors. It's never easy wedging a grown man into a laundry basket.

I drew a deep breath of air and pulled the cupboard doors closed. It was pitch dark inside. After a while, my back felt as if it had gone into spasm. But I knew the discomfort would be worth the wait; it was a small price to pay.

Finally we heard them approach. The door opened a crack. I heard Andy ask, 'A nightcap?' and Shirley's reply in a sultry voice, 'I'll be back in a second.'

Andy entered. From my gap where the two cupboard doors met, I watched him go through to the bathroom and pick up the toothpaste. He placed a blob on his finger, rubbed it across his teeth and swirled his mouth out with water. He was humming, as he ran a comb through his hair. And smiling. I saw him wink at his reflection in the mirror, before turning around and heading back into the bedroom. He switched on the bedside light and switched off the main one. Clearly, he thought tonight was going to be his lucky night. And he hadn't even had to work at it.

There was a knock on the door. Andy opened it and Shirley swanned in. He offered her a drink from the minibar. She sat down on the bed, as he poured the whiskies and sodas. Then he sat down beside her. With his glass in one hand, he ran his fingers of the other hand suggestively down her arm. Shirley responded by leaning in a little closer to him. He didn't need encouragement. In a flash, his arm was around her waist.

As agreed, before we could allow him to embarrass himself any further, we all burst forth out of our hiding places. 'Surprise!' His mortification was palpable. He tried to absolve himself, pretending he had only been playing along by saying, 'Oh, it was all tongue in cheek.' 'Yeah right,' Shirley responded, 'your tongue in my cheek!' Talk about *Schadenfreude* – I was having my fill of it.

The success of this little operation called for celebration. We all dashed back to our rooms to fetch a drink from our own minibars and gathered back in Andy's room. The most relieved person in the saga was Shirley. She realised that the joke could just as easily have been on her, if we had reneged on our part of the bargain to hide in the cupboards.

The next day the crew decided to take me on a cycling trip to the historic wine-growing town of Rudesheim. Most of them had done it before, but it would be my first visit to this atmospheric little tourist town. I'd clearly been sheltered on my previous trips to Germany. It seemed amazing that there were still spots and experiences I hadn't been exposed to. I'd have to mention this to my father, because he was still going on about me having spent enough time in this pointless job. But, to me, it was a further sign that I was nowhere near ready to leave the airline yet for an office career.

It was cold, but not yet snowing, so we dressed up warmly and set off to rent bicycles for the one-way journey. The plan was to return by either train or boat after lunch, since wine-tasting would practically be a prerequisite for the trip.

Always keen for exercise, I couldn't wait to get started. Fortunately, after what ended up being a late night the night before, the journey was not physically demanding. Following the unhurried path through one of the most beautiful parts of Europe, castles were sprinkled on both sides of the Rhine as it provided us with a leisurely, relatively flat journey. The ride was about 40km of exquisite beauty through rolling vineyards and a variety of little villages, where we stopped for a warming cup of coffee as we sat around tables with red-and-white gingham cloths.

Despite the fact that it was the epitome of a tourist town, I found Rudesheim to be picturesque and full of character.

We secured our bicycles to a railing and walked along the famous Drosselgasse, a long, narrow cobblestone street that dated back to the fifteenth century. It was lined with cafés, bars and beer halls. Music and oompah bands filled the air. Now a major tourist attraction, this little street was originally used as a pathway for the fishermen and other sailors on the Rhine, to move between the river and their homes or other destinations.

The Drosskeller was our first stop. The ancient, vaulted wine cellar was imposing and the smell that surrounded us was damp and musty. In typical crew fashion, we tasted every conceivable wine that was offered, but left without buying a single bottle. My excuse was that I didn't really like Riesling.

The choice of restaurants was so large that we simply could not agree. By this stage, I was so hungry I could've eaten a chair leg. Wine-tasting on an empty stomach is never a good idea. Finally, we descended on a quaint little place called Wirtshaus Hannelore, arguably one of the most traditionally German taverns in the town. The inside consisted of wooden booths and a variety of typical, local knick-knacks, giving it a quaint and cosy atmosphere. Our no-nonsense young waiter, clad in lederhosen, resembled a Hitler youth as he rattled off the choice of hearty, regional meats. I was too intimidated to enquire about a vegetarian option. During my short stay in Germany so far, I felt as though I had already consumed an entire wild boar.

If you think German food is all about schnitzel and apple strudel, I've got news for you. They have an appetite for all things swine, especially if it's rich, and unusual enough to produce a gag reflex in someone as uninitiated as me. If hell had a menu, this would've been it. I pored through the list of delicacies, considerately translated for ease of understanding:

Zungenwurst: Blood tongue. The name was enough to force me into an involuntary state of lockjaw. Made from pig's blood, tongue, fat, and if you're lucky, just to ease the guilt-inspired trauma, a touch of oatmeal, or a sprinkling of breadcrumbs, might be added to the mixture.

Speck: Lard. This is pure pig fat. I would sooner have volunteered to eat an entire wax candle than this opaque white grease.

Wiener Wurstchen: Hot dogs. But not made out of 100 per cent meat − I would lay my bottom dollar on these consisting mainly of assholes and eyeballs.

Grubenschmalz: Spreadable pig fat. I wouldn't be surprised if this is what they fed people at assisted suicide clinics, because eating this amounts to an expedited route to the grave.

Sulze: Head cheese. This one has to be the worst of all. Despite its name, this is not a dairy product at all. Instead, it is the meat from the head of a cow or the beloved pig. And this might include the tongue, feet or heart as well. The Germans aren't squeamish. These body parts, which resemble the remains of a bludgeoned-to-death murder victim, then get set in a gelatine and placed in a screw-top jar. Not content with just killing the animal, the poor thing has to be humiliated as well.

Weltmeister Brotchen: World-champion bread roll. This deceptive little item proved to be neither healthy nor edible, as it had enough seeds to choke a kookaburra.

Our waiter did not find humour in the way in which we dissected these epicurean delicacies. He especially didn't find it funny when I discreetly went to the Maître d' and ordered a portion of *Zungenwurst* to be placed directly in front of Shirley. Given the option of choosing between this treat and a cannonball, I'm pretty sure she would have taken her chances on chewing through the steel missile. Despite all of us volunteering to put ten Marks in the kitty for anyone brave enough to taste and swallow a fork full of the disfigured tongue, there were no takers.

Notwithstanding my misgivings, the meal turned out to be delicious. I even managed to coax a salad out of the Gestapo. It was certainly easier getting vegetables out of him than a laugh. I'm sure there are many happy Germans, who spend their entire days laughing until their eyes bulge, just not this one. Or any of the other 4,999 I'd met so far, for that matter.

14

THE BIG BAD APPLE

Three events defined New York in 1989: the Central Park jogger attack, the murder of a young African American male by a crush of white youths and the election of the city's first – and only – black mayor. Crime was rampant, the city was in internal strife fuelled by the quest for money, guns and drugs, notably crack – the cheap, dangerous drug that was intent on destroying the core of the urban population.

On a typical day in 1989, New Yorkers reported nine rapes, five murders, 255 robberies and 19 aggravated assaults. Fear wasn't a knee-jerk reaction; it was a matter of self-preservation. It was scary. 'An under-policed city with crime out of control,' said Dan Rather in his nightly newscast. 'America's capital of racial violence,' said the Reverend Al Sharpton.

It was against this background that Kathy and I arrived in the Big Apple. I had never, on any of my previous trips, developed a passion for this vibrant city, but that didn't stop me from coming back time and time again to give it another bash.

Not because I was a bugger for punishment; the main reason I requested New York flights was due to the layover en route in Ilha do Sal, which I adored. The calm and beauty of that little island was in stark contrast to everything for which New York City stood. I found the sheer scale of it daunting and felt dwarfed by the naked, concrete structures that threatened to engulf and suffocate me. I was the little Tom Thumb of English folklore, forever fighting the gravitational pull of the pavements from the height of tall buildings. Vermin scuttled around the sidewalks, noses to the ground, as if they, too, were overawed by the pace of the city.

I was always quick to spot an opportunity. What this town needed was an operation offering survival skills – the type that require grit, determination and an intent to continue shopping in the face of danger. 'Have you got what it takes to survive New York?' Somebody was going to make money one day.

It was never a good time of the year to be in New York. I was left frigid and desperate in the inhospitable winters, with mucus from my nose frozen solid on my upper lip, and in the summer months dehydrated and fighting for breath, wheezing my way through throngs of angry people as the breeze struggled to find a gap between the myriad skyscrapers.

Even Sir Ranulph Fiennes would have had his work cut out trying to find his way around the city – an intimidating experience, which never improved with repetition. Given the choice, I too, would've opted for crossing both polar ice caps, rather than trying to negotiate my way from one end of the grid to the other. It was fine if you knew that Fifth Avenue divided East from West, so 1 E 34th Street was across the street from 1 W 34th Street, or that the numbers on the streets went up by 100 for each numbered avenue you crossed (with Park

Avenue as 4th Avenue), so from 1 to 99 was from 5th to Park going east and from 5th to 6th going west. 100 to 199 from Park to 3rd or 6th to 7th. On the east side, Madison Avenue was between 5th and Park, Lexington Avenue between Park and 3rd. Do not add 100 for those avenues. On the other hand, the numbers on the avenues had no relation to the street they crossed. For example, 200 5th Avenue was at 23rd Street, but 200 6th Avenue was way downtown, below Houston Street, at Vandam Street. To make matters worse, some avenues had a south section. The correct terminology was 7th Avenue South NOT South 7th Avenue. One more thing – uptown was North and Downtown was South. A solar arctic expedition was beginning to look a lot more attractive.

The incessant racket was an assault on the senses. Either I had been afflicted by a severe case of schizophrenia, or the marginally less-scary alternative was that a little drummer boy had perched himself right inside my ear canal. The noise was constant – police sirens, traffic, burglar alarms and taxi drivers apparently surgically attached to their horns. The people of New York were assertive. I called it loud. Perhaps it was just the trademark accent or maybe it was so that they, too, could be heard above the permanent cacophony of the city. One thing they could certainly do was multitask. It wasn't unusual to see a person walking, talking, eating a wedge of pizza and hailing a yellow cab at the same time, and still muttering out of the side of their mouth.

I soon learnt how to treat New Yorkers. The first rule was to assume that everyone I met was in a hurry. Never make eye contact or smile at a person and always maintain a suspicious attitude toward them. And if you need to ask for directions, keep it short and to the point. On my very first trip to New York,

I was determined to do the tourist thing and experience the thrill of making it to the top of one of the tallest buildings. I hadn't yet learnt the rules of engagement so I'd taken the long-winded, friendly approach. Judging by their responses, the people I intercepted either saw me as a bag lady or a prostitute. Finally, in desperation, when I stopped the next passer-by I asked, 'Excuse me, can you tell me where the Empire State Building is, or should I just go and fuck myself again?' That worked.

How I longed for the sophistication of London, with its aristocratic ways, and the dignified European capitals where people were polite and not pushy. And where food was delivered to your table on a porcelain plate, in manageable portions. And hot coffee did not come in a paper cup. The exception to the latter came the morning we went for breakfast at the local deli. Seated around a horseshoe-shaped counter, a grimy mug was shoved in front of me and a sleep-deprived Irish-American kept filling it up with 'kwoffee' while, at the same time, criticising the way in which I spread cream cheese on my bagel. That's New York for you.

There were two highlights to this trip, one good and one bad. The first one happened in a tiny jazz bar in Greenwich Village. The second was more what one might refer to as an extraordinary experience.

Fat Tuesdays was the epitome of a jazz club in the eighties – tightly packed and hazy with smoke. Six of us sat around a small table, with a medley of frozen margaritas and beers, as we waited for the entertainment to begin.

I couldn't help but overhear the conversation at the small table beside me. The man was clearly an out-of-towner, who had found himself in New York at the height of the tourist season and had decided to revisit this little jazz pub, which he'd obviously been to before. He was also desperate for a drink and kept flailing his arms about, trying to get the attention of the overworked waiter. Finally, he managed to catch the server's eye and took the amiable route, trying to engage him in conversation. 'You know, it's been over five years since I first came in here.' With a deadpan face and in typical New York style, the waiter replied, 'I'm sorry, Sir, but you'll have to wait your turn. I can only serve one table at a time.' I have a finely tuned ear for sarcasm.

I had no idea who was going to be performing in Fat Tuesdays that night. I wasn't a massive jazz fan, so wasn't au fait with the who's who of the jazz world, but even I couldn't fail to recognise the trumpeter with the trademark swollen cheeks. I was delirious with excitement to be seeing Dizzy Gillespie in the flesh – one of the greatest jazz trumpeters of all time. He placed the instrument to his lips and puffed out his cheeks. If ever I found myself in a situation where I had to hide two footballs, as one does, I knew exactly who to call on. Not only were his abnormally large cheeks enough to define this most revered jazz artist, but another symbol of his remarkable career was his signature 'bent' trumpet. This design was brought about by accident. He told us the story, 'On one auspicious night in 1953, things got a little rowdy at a birthday party for my lovely wife. An innocent pair of dancers tripped over my instrument, where it stood on its stand in a corner during a break. As a result, the bell was bent. But I had a job to do – I had to finish the performance, so I picked it up, played on, and discovered that I liked the sound of the banged-up instrument.' It projected better over the heads of the audience. And that was that. Ever since that night, whenever he got a new trumpet, it was specially designed for him with the bell bent at forty-five degrees.

He was a born entertainer. I couldn't help but love this man with the huge personality and playful presence. He was like everybody's favourite grandfather.

It didn't end there. The curtains parted, and stepping out to join him on the small stage was the crooner, Tony Bennett, well-known singer of works by George Gershwin, Irving Berlin and Cole Porter. It was quite incredible being in such an intimate environment with these two world-famous jazz personalities, who were close enough for me to reach out and touch.

They were in no rush to get off the stage. Their ability to connect with the crowd was legendary and it felt as if they were playing and singing for me alone. I am convinced that even if they did not earn a dime that night, it wouldn't have mattered one bit to them.

That had to be karma. For someone who disliked New York as much as I did, I ended up having one of the most memorable evenings of my life.

It was time to make our way back to the hotel. Not an easy feat around midnight. Catching a taxi in New York is mandatory, but never easy. It's nothing like the fictitious, classic New York movie, where a guy in a crisp business suit throws an arm out and yells, 'Taxi' and a yellow cab instantly appears. In fact, it's the polar opposite. You have to practically fling yourself into the middle of the street, flailing about like a hapless jellyfish just to be noticed. And still, they will avoid you with the determination of a vegetarian at a cattle market. But it is an experience as quintessentially American as eating a burger from a cart, or getting lost in Central Park – sometimes good, but mostly bad.

On our second afternoon in New York, Kathy and I went shopping. Now I need to tell you something about my friend Kathy: she could shop. She actually liked traipsing around for hours trying on every conceivable outfit known to mankind. And no matter if she didn't really even like the look of it, she'd walk all the way to the far side of the warehouse just to touch something. I remember her husband once saying to me that the reason they always walked around the streets – at home, on holiday, on business trips – holding hands, had absolutely nothing to do with romance; it was simply because he knew without any doubt whatsoever, that the minute he let go of her hand, she would shop. She could find a pair of shoes in a fish shop.

Even if it was her fifteenth time in London and Buck House was beginning to look a bit jaded and like it could do with a lick of paint, or the Great Pyramids of Giza were starting to resemble a melting Toblerone, in contrast, the shops always looked shiny and new. Where some people were born to dance or sing, Kathy was born to shop. If she went window-shopping, she'd probably come home with the windows. She justified this frenzy as form of exercise, convinced that she sometimes even lost weight during a particularly enthusiastic shopping spree. Until I pointed out to her that the only thing that weighed substantially less after one of her outings, was her purse.

Perhaps I was not a real hostie because, to me, shopping was a bit of a chore. Look, I could force myself to amble round a mall from time to time, or haggle at the markets in Hong Kong, but I had no interest in forging long-term relationships with Donna Karan, Calvin Klein or Ralph Lauren. Even the temptation of a life-changing markdown on a sale rack, was not enough to lure me. A lot of hosties flew from city to city, their main ambition, to bag a bargain. I would see them staggering back to the hotel, shopping bags attached to the end of their arms like dumbbells, buckled knees hovering just above shiny new Jimmy Choos. They could spend an entire week in Paris with no food, investing their whole meal allowance in clothing, make-up and jewellery, instead. Women went shopping, men payed rugby – both qualified as contact sports. You were just less likely to get trampled to death in a game of rugby. And the competitors were less sweaty.

Being the good friend that I was, I had accompanied my friend Kathy on so many shopping trips that they generally blurred into each other. I also feared going shopping with her, knowing that even I would be lured into allowing vast sums of plastic money to pass through my fingers. Credit cards were like mosquitos. You could keep them at bay for a while, but sooner or later, they came back to suck your blood.

However, the reason I remember this specific spending-spree is due to the perseverance she displayed in getting what she wanted. That day, I learnt something about achieving your goals. We had spotted a dummy in a shop window, draped in an elegant black maxi-coat. Both of us wanted one. We stepped inside and tried on the appropriate sizes. The cool satin lining tickled my arms and the cashmere was soft, as I ran my palms over it. They were gorgeous; we had to have them. I hauled out a credit card and paid for my purchase with the satisfaction of one who has just managed to make an omelette out of a Faberge egg. Kathy proffered her card; it was declined. The shopkeeper tried again; same story – the amount was too high. Unabashed, Kathy instructed the woman to run the card through in increments of five dollars at a time. We were in for a long ride. After each successful transaction, all three of us whooped for joy. Nineteen transactions later and the coat was hers.

We were ambling around somewhere in the Upper East Side, when we heard what sounded like a shot. Not really familiar with the severity of the crime situation in the city, we didn't pay it that much attention. Or perhaps, due to the high levels of constant unrest in our own home country, we were slightly blunted to the wild-west effects of these regular occurrences. Undeterred, we continued perusing the shop windows.

However, a few more shots rang out, people started running around and a slight panic ensued, so we thought it might be an opportune time to look for shelter. We ducked into a dark building, which turned out to be a restaurant, and moved as far to the back as we could. It seemed empty, probably due to the fact that it was somewhere between lunch and dinner time. Huddled together, hearts pounding, we could hear the muted voices of people screaming outside amidst police sirens, but that was pretty much my interpretation of New York so I didn't think it terribly out of the ordinary. Nonetheless, call me a coward, but I was happy to be safely tucked into the bowels of an anonymous abyss.

We stayed still in there for a while, talking in whispers, as the noise outside showed signs of abating. Then, since all seemed well, we figured that as we were hungry, we might as well stay there and eat. It was a restaurant, after all. We'd wait out whatever it was that had been going on in the street, until total calm had been restored. So we sat ourselves down at one of the tables and looked around for a waiter. After a short while, a startled looking chap came along with menus. There was a sense of urgency about him as he scribbled down our order, meticulously avoiding eye contact. Our poor garcon was filled with a kind of crippling anxiety and discomfort that could only result in loose bowels. He looked like the type who would be frightened by the sounds of crickets and birds chirping. Maybe he was just a regular New Yorker. It didn't occur to us that we were the only patrons. And he was the only waiter.

We chatted our way through salads and iced tea, oblivious to life on the outside, until the lure of the shops got the better of Kathy and we called for the bill. The shifty-eyed waiter took our money and ushered us towards the door, before skulking back to the cavernous depths of the building.

Preparing ourselves for the glare of daylight, we stepped outside, only to discover that our exit was barred by reams of yellow tape. The police had cordoned off the entire block, keeping everyone out and we were inside the sealed-off area. I didn't have a clue what was going on, but I had an overwhelming need to escape. All there was for us to do was to duck underneath the tape. Not as easy as that. A cop yelled at us, 'Get back!'

'What do you mean?' I asked.

'You can't climb under the tape like that!'

'Well, how are we supposed to get out?'

'You shouldn't have been inside a crime scene to begin with. How did you get in there?'

'Crime scene??!! We were just eating in a restaurant, and you put the tape up while we were inside.'

'That's impossible. We checked all the businesses on the block before we put up the tape.'

'Well, you couldn't have checked very well. We were right there, inside that building. And so was a waiter.'

'You couldn't have been.'

'We were. How do we get out of here?'

'Get out the way you came in.'

'This is the way we got in,' I said, pointing at the tape.

He could obviously see that we were not part of the mafia. He turned his back and let us slip under the tape unnoticed.

Such was the yin and the yang of New York in the '80s – from an enchanting evening with Dizzy Gillespie one day, to be caught up in a crime scene the next.

15

JOURNEY'S END

February 1993

Disillusionment is a wicked thing. Nobody wants to see the fantasy end. I remember, as a child, when the magician pulled that final rabbit out of his hat and the show was over, we all had to go home, back to normality, back to boring old life.

That is how I felt on the morning of the first day of February in 1993. Nothing had prepared me for the epiphany that was about to end one existence and begin another. I just hadn't seen it coming. There was no sudden intuitive insight, no single event or occurrence that led me to the realisation that it was time for me to leave the airline.

I simply woke up that day, disappointed to discover that my life was no longer quite as good as I'd always believed it to be. It might have had something to do with the fact that when I put on the familiar uniform and looked at myself in the mirror, the face that stared back at me was no longer youthful and unlined.

Experience was etched all over it. Some may call them 'crow's feet'; I prefer to regard them as 'laughter lines'. Because that's how I got them. Let's forget genetics for the time being. Damn, age is a high price to pay for maturity!

I applied my make up with the same fervour as always, but the unpleasant truth was that youth and looks are transient, reserved for the young. This was a lifestyle that could not be sustained forever, a vacuous world of glamour and frivolity. How I'd loved it! I'd travelled to places that many people had only ever read about. I'd made good friends and lost good friends. I'd learnt about other worlds and cultures, eaten strange foods and witnessed foreign traditions.

I had entered the airline in 1983 as a naïve young graduate, with my newly acquired degree tucked firmly into the bottom drawer of my desk. And my bottom tucked firmly into the pencil skirt of my newly acquired uniform. I had blushed at the sound of a swear word and felt disarmed by the attempted seductions of men. My innocent upbringing had not quite prepared me for the life into which I had chosen to throw myself. And yet, by the same token, it had been my salvation.

The clodhopping hillbilly of my youth was a chasm away from the unshockable sophisticate I had grown into. Now, I'm not for one moment suggesting that the path I had travelled to reach that point was a virtuous one, but it had certainly incorporated a lot of fun. I looked, with a mixture of pity and envy, upon my childhood friends, who went through life as blinkered as competitors in a steeplechase. They would never ask for more out of life, but neither would they feel cheated or disappointed by it.

It was not only my level of emotional maturity that had grown over this ten-year period. So, too, had my vast collection of disposable plastic shower caps, miniature emery boards and shoe-polishing kits. To a grand total of 3,427 sets, to be exact. Not to mention the 576 pairs of slumber shades, a supply large enough to start a hotel chain, which added to my realisation that perhaps it was an opportune time to start contemplating my future in the real world. After all, my professional achievements during this period could probably be inscribed on the nib of a ballpoint pen.

It was on this morning that I knew I wanted more out of life. I instinctively felt the time had come for me to take up the challenge of embarking on the next phase. I had grown comfortable in this easy-come, easy-go environment, but this was not how or where I wanted my career, or my future, for that matter, to end. The realisation that I was ten years older, hit me with the force of a meteor entering a black hole. I wanted to start a new career, and at 32 I didn't have the luxury of time to waste. Much as I loved him, I wasn't doing this for my poor, disappointed father. To be fair, he didn't really object to the occupation that had consumed ten years of my life. He'd obviously made his peace with it. He was well aware of the educational benefits of travel, though hopefully less aware of the many other educational benefits I had picked up along the way. I was doing it for ME.

It would've been easy to allow myself to be trapped in that flippant existence of no-strings-attached travel, romance and fun. But I could see it for what it was. Transient. I had finally reached the stage where I wanted more than this farcical life. My youthful fascination with smart uniforms had run its course. I now longed for boardrooms and business suits. And a tad of mental stimulation would not go amiss, either. Ironically, I craved normality and routine, the very lack of which had drawn me to this job in the first place. I yearned to be home with my family at Christmas time. Enough missed weddings and other important events. The reality is that life presents itself with a number of opportunities and I didn't want to stand accused of forfeiting a single one of these. It was time to move on to the next challenge. As someone once said, 'If at first you didn't succeed, then at least you'd know that skydiving wasn't for you.' Wise words. A bit late, though. There were goals to be set and achieved. I wanted a career, a proper grown-up job where I would be taken seriously. I wanted to be asked if I was a member of a select corporate club, not a member of the seedy mile-high club.

I wasn't at a crossroads. It was time to leave. My decision was as clear as if I'd been paid a visit by the Holy Ghost. I had been privileged to experience a snippet of life that very few would ever be exposed to and had grasped it with both hands, albeit an intoxicating, but temporary, make-believe world. As required, I had signed up for the obligatory two years, but found myself in the airline eight years more than that, without regretting a single second of it. It had undoubtedly been the very best period of my young life, but I was grateful for the solid moral footing with which I had entered that ambiguous environment. Without that stable basis, I might easily have fallen victim to the less salubrious side of this rusty coin.

An extraordinary, prodigious and marvellous lifestyle, there was also a sordid side to life in the airlines. It took a fair amount of resilience not to succumb to the pitfalls of this seductive mode of living, which preyed like quicksand on the vulnerable and fractured personalities that made up this libertine sector of people. Life in the airline was a challenge, with many hazards to guard against, cleverly disguised as recreation.

The biggest demon was drink. A lot of people in this work environment believed that a balanced diet was a bottle of wine in each hand. We all lived by the indisputable misconception that alcohol was proof that God loved us and wanted only for us to be happy. But, in truth, alcohol abuse was rife amongst the cabin crew and, rightly or wrongly, we all protected colleagues from exposure. Back then, employers did not offer the option of emotional support to loyal, but possibly troubled, workers. Counselling, if deemed necessary, was something you did entirely on your own. As long as you recognised the wake-up call in time to avoid getting fired for either being drunk, or caught drinking on duty. To many of those plagued souls, eventually dependent on alcohol for their everyday existence, it was a marvel that they continued to function in this work environment, with the hideous temptation forever at their fingertips. They constantly battled against the torment of being enclosed in a capsule, filled with trolley upon trolley of miniature bottles of alcohol, for up to eleven hours at a time. Some of them capitulated. It was easy to be critical, but I always remembered the wise words spoken by a kind man, 'Before you criticise somebody, you need to walk a mile in their shoes.' I wondered if this was out of compassion or self-preservation, as then you'd be a mile away from this drunk and aggressive person and they'd be barefoot.

Occasionally, exposure and the consequences thereof were unavoidable. It would have been impossible to have concealed the actions of an inebriated colleague who opened the aircraft door on landing, before the stairs were in place at the mouth of the exit. He promptly stepped into thin air and fell approximately 4m to the ground, where he lay in a crumpled mess. An ambulance was called and the disembarking of the passengers was delayed, both resulting in a significant cost to the airline. He survived the fall, but it was not a good career move. His services were terminated, before he even left hospital. Rehab was for his own account.

The other sadness was the onset of AIDS. Throughout the 1980s, it was closely linked to homosexuality in the minds of many. In South Africa, with its conservative Calvinistic attitudes at the time, the airline had become a haven for gay men. It was simply a fact that most of the stewards were gay. And happy to be able to have found an environment where they could be themselves, without being continually judged for it. Sadly, however, some of these young men came from staunch Afrikaner backgrounds, where homosexuality was so taboo that they were either disinherited or completely banished from their families, unless they were prepared to conform to some sort of semblance of 'normality'. To many of them, the airline was an escape and it also provided them with the freedom of sexual promiscuity. And were they promiscuous! Sex was not the answer. It was the question, but YES was always the answer.

In January 1983, one of the celebrated South African newspapers led with the headline, 'Homosexual disease kills SAA staff', exposing the fact that two South African Airways stewards had died after apparently becoming the country's first casualties of the malady that affected mainly homosexuals and drug addicts.

The early years of AIDS brought with it a great fear and anxiety for gay men everywhere, mostly generated by the mysterious and lethal nature of this hitherto unknown condition. In addition to this, was the homophobia whipped up by the sensation-seeking media and the sustained use of the terms 'gay plague' and 'gay bug' when referring to the disease.

Not only was it the gay men who were anxious about this mysterious ailment. In the airline, we all sat up and took notice. In fact, we were scared. Nobody knew just how the virus was passed on. People speculated about being sneezed on, spat on, touching the saliva, or even a tear from an infected person leading to contracting the disease. On board, we all worked in such close proximity and even shared bunks and bed linen in the crew rest. What about bugs or mosquitos – could they not transmit the illness? If any of the above theories proved to be true, we were all damned. Many crew members started bringing their own sleeping bags along. It was a tough time. Nobody wanted to appear callous, but the survival instinct overruled all else and so we kept our physical distance as far as possible, without causing offence. If only we'd known then that only direct sexual contact and shared hypodermic needles could pass on this nasty sickness. My chest aches when I think about the rejection so many poor souls had to put up with when a hug would have meant so much.

Passengers were sometimes less compassionate, as they refused to be served by an obviously gay and possibly ill-looking steward. There was no protocol. But the airline couldn't risk losing passengers, so the minute a crew member got ill and displayed the obvious symptoms, they were grounded.

AIDS had everything – sex, celebrity exposés, moral enterprise, conspiracy theories and the opportunity to kick a group that was already marginalised from mainstream society. It allowed religious zealots to conclude that gay lifestyles actually generated AIDS as God's punishment. Very little was known about the transmission of the virus and hence the gay community was further ostracised.

There is little doubt that AIDS was first detected in gay men and, for a brief period, desperate researchers examined the so-called gay lifestyle for clues as to causation. By 1983, it was clear that AIDS was a global issue that was affecting different groups in different countries. Studies coming out of Africa were showing that AIDS had been around long before its emergence in the West.

Whatever the cause and facts surrounding the AIDS issue, the reality was that I was losing friends and colleagues to it. It was soul-destroying time and time again to witness the onset of the general malaise, flaky skin and massive weight loss as the virus took hold. In typical South African disaster management tradition, humour was used to cushion the despair. Each time a new victim was afflicted by this grim disease, it was referred to as a visit from Aunty Aida. Both my very dearest colleagues from my early days of flying – Mani da Souza and Barry – have since been paid this visit. My memories of them and the effect they both had on my airline experiences will always claim a very special corner in my heart.

The effects of AIDS should have had a curtailing effect on romance, but life in the airline continued its enigmatic path, with little regard for reality. Despite a constant flurry of flirtation, dalliance and a light dusting of passion, I had reached the conclusion that the pursuit of long-term romantic happiness in this environment had become another area of malcontent. People always told me that someday my Prince Charming would come along. Mine obviously took a wrong turning, got lost and was too stubborn to ask for directions. I would have to hunt him down on my own. Outside of the airline.

The general public had a fanciful perception of love in the airline, with a glamorous air hostess lacing a gloved hand through the crooked elbow of her pilot companion. What they didn't factor in was that, generally only one of these was unencumbered.

While we all turned a blind eye to affairs of the heart, conventional or otherwise, there was no long-term pleasure to be gained in extra-marital relationships, which, it has to be said, were not much of a challenge to conduct in any airline. Ultimately, there was always a loser somewhere in the equation. Occasionally a family was torn apart but, more often, a young woman with much to offer, and who had given her entire youth to a man she loved, was cast aside on the very same day that he finally retired. There were many of these emotionally fragmented and bitter senior bags in the airline. Perhaps they lived by the adage that it was better to have loved and lost than never to have loved at all. I knew that I wanted more from life.

As I made my way to the admin building to officially fill out a form and hand in my resignation, happy memories barged their way into my consciousness. I recalled a recent flight where, on handing out the specially requested meals, I found myself with a foil container labelled 'VGML'. Smiling at the bearded gentleman sitting in the corresponding seat, before placing the meal in front of him, I asked, 'Are you vegetarian, sir?' He looked startled, waved his hands in the air and replied, 'No, Ma'am. I'm Jordanian.'

Another memory was one of being on Ilha do Sal over New Year. In my unbiased opinion, there could be no better place to see in the New Year. The hotel staff had excelled themselves and lunch on the first of January was a magnificent affair. They tripped over themselves to be of service. They tripped over each other. They tripped over the furniture. Alcohol might have been involved; it was New Year, after all. We gathered in the dining-room for the feast. On display, heading up the buffet, was a scrumptious-looking suckling pig – probably the only one on the island, specially bred for this occasion, only to be defaced with a cigarette in its lifeless mouth and a pair of Ray Bans perched upon its porcine face. No event would be complete without the crew leaving their mark.

Air travel has come a long way, but not necessarily all for the better. On the positive side, there are a gazillion more flights and routes to choose from, airfares have dropped due to competition and travel agents have just about become obsolete. The excitement of planning a trip, discussing it over an atlas, maps and brochures at the agency and finally coming home with a travel wallet full of cardboard encased air tickets, brings back a sense of nostalgia. A far cry from the way we do it now, seated at a desk in front of a computer for a quick comparison between a multitude of low-cost airlines, before hitting the 'confirm and pay' button. As easy as that. And as soulless. Retrieving a boarding pass on your smartphone is not quite the same as gathering passports, air tickets and inoculation certificates prior to leaving for the airport. It's enough to make me curl up and weep for my lost youth.

As air crew in those days, we didn't require visas. Even as South Africans. We were issued with 'official passports' and went through the same channels as diplomatic passport holders, which meant that we weren't liable to any sort of security searches, either. Not that security was a big thing, then. Both passengers and crew simply walked through a doorframe-like metal detector. If it buzzed, a security guard would ask if you had a dangerous weapon on your person. This is the point at which most South African males would swagger and growl, 'Well, I do have a dangerous weapon on me, but not one I can show in public!' Nudge, nudge, wink, wink. The embarrassed security guard would giggle and let them pass through, without any further checks.

There were no laptops or iPhones that needed to be placed in bins. We all wedged alcohol and other liquids, in large quantities, protectively into our carry-on hand luggage. No one was forced to practise a striptease routine before passing through security. Shoes remained firmly on our feet. Jackets and coats were kept on. We didn't even have to take off our belts. And the entire process did not result in lengthy queues of people trying to dress themselves and gather their belongings in a frantic rush, as the big, plastic bins piled up quicker than a tsunami. Fellow passengers did not glare at us as we struggled, with clumsy fingers, to pull thigh-high boots back to where they had been comfortably located before. The whole process today is enough to scar even the most hard-core exotic dancer. It's a bit like playing strip poker, or feathers, with about 400,000 strangers, all in a mad scramble to catch a plane.

Those were the days when families accompanied their loved ones all the way to the boarding gate and then stood and watched the plane take off through the huge plate-glass windows. The terminals were bright, clean and practically empty. Flying was such an occasion that people dressed in their finest gear, airline food was enticing and air hostesses were happy to see passengers. It all seems very remote now. I would like to be able to say that even the check-in staff were happy, but that would be a step too far. Never have been, never will be. They wouldn't qualify for the job otherwise.

My parents were ecstatic to hear that I was considering a 'proper' job. I just couldn't commit to when. There was one huge hurdle when it came to leaving the airline, and that was leaving the airline. It was hard to imagine a life outside of this hedonistic existence and the easy, undemanding friendships that constituted it. Parting from this close-knit fraternity would be like what I could only imagine instituting divorce proceedings with a long-term partner, would be like. To voluntarily sever this umbilical cord surely bordered on insanity. Was I mad to let the pursuit of future personal growth stand in the path of current happiness?

I never shed a tear as I retraced my steps to the car park at the Cabin Services Building. My bag bulged with experiences and memories to last a lifetime. I had made special friends, who would always be part of my future.

As a headstrong young girl, I had been seduced by the glamour of the job. I had fallen for the allure of travel and fun. Forgive me for thinking that those were the 'good old days' – I was in my 20s, moderately attractive to men, and I thrived on the attention. I would have been insulted had I not been the one selected to have my boobs fondled for a 100 rand. I might even have considered doing it for nothing. I look back now on those days, with rose-tinted glasses. It was a different world, but it wasn't necessarily better. It was just acceptable, because that's the way it was. I have been left fortified by that life and the lessons I learnt. Never again would I allow myself to be flattered by the lascivious attention of menfolk … mainly because I haven't had the opportunity. Age is a terrible thing. Flying is for the birds.

Clearly, nostalgia is not a patch on what it used to be.

———————————————— ✈